MEAL PREP

A journey through healthy and tasty meals for weight loss and clean eating

By
Nola Rowan

Copyright ©

All rights reserved.

This document is geared towards providing exact and reliable information in regards to the topic and issue covered.

No part of this book may be reproduced in any form or by any electronic or mechanical means including information storage and retrieval systems, without permission in writing from the author. The exception is by reviewer, who may quote short excerpts in a review.

The trademarks that are used are without any consent, and the publication of the trademark is without permission or backing by the trademark owner. All trademarks and brands within this book are for clarifying purposes only and are owned by the owners themselves, not affiliated with this document.

TABLE OF CONTENTS

Introduction 9
Create Your Meal Plan 12
Preparing For Meal Prep 12
Foods You Shouldn't Refrigerate 13
Foods You Can Refrigerate, But Don't Need To 13
Things You Should Always Refrigerate 14
Buying Fresh And Local 15
Stocking 15
Oils And Vinegars 15
Condiments, Sauces, And Other Flav 16
Nuts, Seeds, And Dried Fruits 17
Grains 17
In The Freezer 18
Shrimp 18
The Spice Rack 18
Which Fruits And Vegetables? 18
Food To Eat Each Season 19
Winter 19
Spring 21
Summer 23
Fall 24
Conversion Table 27
Perfect-Start Smoothie 29
Peach Smoothie 30
Cereza With Vanilla - Smoothie 31
Espresso Smoothie 32
Chesse-Fruit Tortilla 33

Sea Fruits Sandwich	34
Hell Combo Sandwich	35
Peanut Butter And Banana Mix	37
Autumn Spread With Honey	38
Sweet Pudding With Fruits	39
Oatmeal With Vanilla Flavour	40
Bran Muffins	41
Egg With Surprise	45
Turkey Egg With Asparagus	47
Grande Burrito	48
Grilled Portobello Mushrooms	50
Eggs With Salmon And Golden Onion	51
Pumpernickel Crisps	52
Healthy Breakfast With Broccoli	53
Sweet French Toast	54
Tasty French Toast Bake	56
Pancake With Peach	57
Peach Compote With Maple Syrup	58
Whole-Wheat Fruit Pancakes With Nutty Topping	59
Almonds Topping	61
Honey Quinoa	61
Exotic Chicken Salad	64
Lemon-Cumin Grilled Chicken	65
Sourish Chicken Breast	67
Poached Chicken Breast	68
Pasta Salad	68
Salad A La Nice	70
Beef Taco Salad With Tomato Dressing	71

Multicolor Salad	73
Greek Salad With Chicken And Feta	74
Thailand Chicken	76
Crunchy Chicken	77
Mediterranean Sea Fruits	78
Steak Beef Sandwich With Herbs And Tasty Sauce	80
Tuna Stuffed With Fresh Herbs	82
Shrimp Soup-Cream	83
Ravioli-Spinach Soup	84
Prosciutoo & Cheese Sandwich	88
Greek Pizza With Lamb And Salad	90
Fennel-Arugula Salad	92
Pizza All-In	93
Spaghetti Omlette With Salad Presto	94
Salad Presto	96
Chicken Paillard With Herbs & Tomato Salad	96
Grilled Beef With Apple Salad	98
Strawberry And Cheese Salad	99
Club Salad	101
Crab And Avocado Combo With Cool Cucumber Soup	103
Fresh Cucumber Soup	104
Shrimp Roll With Cracked Spicy Potato Chips	105
Cracked And Spicy Pepper Potato Chips	107
Chicken Cheesy Sandwich	107
Multi-Color Pepper Steak	111
Russian Beef With Fresh Green Beans And Grainy Mustard	112
Fresh Green Beans And Grainy Mustard	114
Emerald Chao-Bao With Beef	114

Steak Chimichurri With Garlic Bruschetta And Tomatoes	116
Bruschetta	119
Grilled Tomatoes	120
Extra Burger With Olives And Creamy Broccoli Salad	120
Creamy Broccoli Salad	122
Exotic Pork Stir-Fry	122
Steak Pork Piccata With Spinach And Mashed Potatoes With Garlic	125
Express " Steamed " Spinach	127
Mashed Potatoes With Garlic	127
Mediterranean Glazed Pork With Maple Squash Puree And Spinach-Green	128
Maple Squash Puree	129
Spinach-Green	131
Chicken-Mushroom Tortilla	132
Barbecue Chicken Sandwiches With Classic Coleslaw	134
Classic Coleslaw	136
Tasty Peach Chicken	137
Chicken With Tomato-Corn Mix	139
Panzanella With Spicy Chicken Sausage	141
Flaky Flounder With Almond Topping, Saffron Rice, And Citrus Broccolini	143
Saffron Rice	144
Citrus Broccolini	145
Shrimp With Garlic And Basil	146
Salmon With Chickpea Ragu And Lemon	147
Prosciutto Crudo-Wrapped Salmon With Pesto Potatoes And Green Beans	149
Pesto Potatoes And Green Beans	150
Mussels Provencal With Trio Salad	151
Trio Salad	152
Sesame Shrimp With Rice And Cabbage	153

Spring Pasta	154
Asian Noodle Mix	156
Shrimp Fra Diavolo A La Popeye	158
Mint Penne With Zucchini	160
Pasta With Crab And Asparagus	161
Simple Ravioli Toss	163
Entrecote Steak With Mustard Sauce And Parmesan Steak "Fries"	166
Parmesan Steak " Fries "	168
Porcini Crusted Filet Mignon With Herbed Potatoes And Creamed Spinach	169
Herbed Mashed Potatoes	170
Creamed Spinach With Shallots And Nutmeg Powder	171
Herbed Beef Stew With Butternut Squash	172
Aromatic Steak With Cheese Sauce	174
Baked Beans With Ham And Citrus Cabbage Salad	176
Citrus Cabbage Salad	177
Ham-Wrapped Endive Tart And Green Salad With Shallot Vinaigrette	178
Paella With Chorizo And Green Olives	180
Chicken And Grape Skewers With Lentils	182
Lentils Pilaf	183
Aromatic Turkey With Roasted Potatoes And Brussels Sprouts	185
Roasted Potatoes	187
Brussels Sprouts	187
Simple Turkey Chili	188
Classic Tuna Noodle Casserole	190
Ratatouille With Fresh Red Snapper And Herbed Goat Cheese Crostini	192
Herbed Goat Cheese Crostini	193
Salmon Marianted In Tomato Sauce With Swiss Chard	195
Salmon Milanese With Quinoa Pilaf	197

Sweet Combo Cluster 200

Dried Fruit With Chocolate Topping 201

Powdered Coconut-Sugar Crisps 202

Chocolate-Covered Cheese Panini Bites 203

Honeydew Soup With Lemon-Raspberry Sorbet 206

Oranges Dipped In Honey With Toasted Hazelnuts 207

Spicy Pineapple 209

Pears Dipped In Almond Cream 210

Fruit Salad With Mint And Honey-Lime Dressing 211

Bbq Peaches With Ice Cream 213

Fast Cake With Mango Sauce 214

Crispy Rice Treats With Dried Fruits 217

Aromatic Truffles With Figs 218

Simple Lemon Bars 219

Cobbler With Lime-Berries 221

Big Apple 223

Raspberry Tart 224

Halloween Pudding 225

Ricotta Cream With Strawberries Syrup 228

Sparkling Peaches Cocktail 230

C"H"Oco-Nut On Stick 231

Summer-Vibes Pops 232

Ice Cream Packed 233

INTRODUCTION

Meal prep is a simple routine that will forever change your life.

As a nation, we are growing smarter and smarter about our food choices. Never before have there been so many significant resources for health-minded families.

However, knowing is only half the battle right? Execution is the other half. And many of us still face problems choosing healthy alternatives for our daily meals.

When it comes to healthy eating, preparation is key to your success. One study published in the American Journal of Preventative Medicine suggests that spending time on preparing and cooking meals at home is linked to better dietary habits.

As an alternative to quitting your takeout habits cold turkey, you can trick yourself by preparing meals ahead of time and conveniently packaging them for easy reheating. When you feel like running out to get a cold-cut calorie bomb instead you'll have a hearty stash of tummy friendly meals at your disposal. You can pull out something like this and heat it faster than running out to your favorite fast food spot saving time and also money!

It's not easy to choose healthy foods when you lead a busy life — and let's face it, we all lead busy lives.

Learning how to meal prep correctly will not only save you time and energy, but it will also help to make sure that you and your family eat homemade and nutritious meals. Providing practical and simple solutions with easy to follow instructions, The Meal Prep Cookbook shows you how simple it is to enjoy fresh and flavorful meals on even the most hectic days.

This book is full of solutions in the form of delicious, inspired recipes that provide the answer to every meal call of the week - all in the most effortless way possible. This is more than a collection of recipes, it is a little peace of mind and a lot of satisfaction. It is peace of mind knowing that no matter what life dishes out, or your level of confidence in the kitchen, you have the tools you need to nourish yourself and your family. And it is the ultimate satisfaction that comes from indulging in incredible, fortifying food every day.

That's what makes Meal Prepping so great.

If you are tired of dieting with no results, it's time to ditch the fad diets and start meal prepping. Here are three more reasons why you want to start meal prepping if you aren't doing so already: frui

- ✓ Get results quicker - Meal prep, when performed correctly, is accurate. You are eating the right foods in the right quantities. Having a meal plan is a great start, but when you go all the way to ensure that you're measuring all your ingredients and then portioning them out, you will notice quicker results. You don't guess how much to eat. You are eating what you're supposed to be eating.

- ✓ Save time - Although you need to carve out a good two to three hours to meal prep on Sundays (or whatever day works best for you), doing all your cooking in one chunk of time is more efficient. You will save time since you only have to prepare your kitchen, cook, and clean once (or a few times) per week.

- ✓ Stop cheating - By preparing your meals in advance, you are less likely to cheat on your meal plan. Meal prep will keep you on track to reach your goals. And even if you don't tend to eat junk food, portioning your meals will stop you from overeating. Remember, overeating healthy food is still overeating.

WHAT IS MEAL PREP?

Meal Prepping merely is preparing some, or all of your meals ahead of time. It's like having those TV dinners that you would purchase from the store, except that you prepare them yourself, with better, healthier and unprocessed ingredients.

Not only does it save you time, but it also helps to ensure you eat healthier foods more often with the proper portions, instead of reaching for quick processed and prepackaged snacks or meals that go over your caloric needs.

The idea is that when you have healthier things ready to eat, you will eat them instead of other potentially harmful foods. And it works incredibly well.

CREATE YOUR MEAL PLAN

Before you get started with meal prep, you need to plan out the meals that you'll be preparing. At it's most simple, this consists of finding recipes that you like and that satisfy your nutritional requirements. Remember the saying, failing to plan is planning to fail. It's time to execute!

PREPARING FOR MEAL PREP

More than hundred recipes organized into chapters that provide the solution to every possible mealtime situation. There are simple pick and go breakfasts for days when you are prone to skip this important meal, as well as easy breakfast options for when you have a little more time or want to overwhelm your guests. There are lunches to go, with simple packing instructions to ensure that lunch is something to look forward to wherever you are. And there are at-home lunches for when you have the time of eating in. There are rush-hour dinners - fabulous meals you can whip up in less than thirty minutes without breaking a sweat - as well as dinners for days when you have a bit more time to marinate or roast, but still, want it all to be effortless. Finally, there are decadent desserts, some ready in minutes and others truly worth waiting for, all effortlessly pulled together.

FOODS YOU SHOULDN'T REFRIGERATE

- Potatoes: The cold temperatures in your fridge will turn potatoes' starch into sugars, giving it a sweet flavor when you cook them (and not in a good way). These can be stored at room temperature.

- Tomatoes: If you've tried this, you probably know why Tomatoes shouldn't be stored in the fridge. They get mushy and gross. Leave them out.

- Honey: A lot of people put honey in the fridge, but this will thicken it up to something fierce, and it doesn't require refrigeration to stay good. Unless you like your honey cold, you can put this in the pantry.

- Onions: Onions will last longer in the fridge, but not without cost. Like tomatoes, your onions will soften a bit if you put them in the fridge, and they won't be quite as crisp. Also, they'll make your other food smell like onions. Keep them out of the fridge at room temperature, and away from your potatoes—proximity can make the onions go bad quicker!

FOODS YOU CAN REFRIGERATE, BUT DON'T NEED TO

- Peanut Butter: Sure, you could...but why? Apart from some organic varieties, you can keep peanut butter in the pantry, and it'll be fine. Not to mention it'll be easier to spread.

- Bread: If you leave bread in the fridge, it'll start to get a tougher texture, which isn't always desirable. That said, you can store it in the fridge if you can't eat it fast enough before it goes bad—I'd much prefer my bread a tad rougher than have to throw half of it out.

- Bananas: Most people store these outside of the fridge, which is fine. If you put them in the fridge, they'll turn black, but the insides will still be fine.

> Baked Goods: Like bread, chilling baked goods will make them last longer, but at a small cost: they'll go stale faster. Unless they contain some filling that requires refrigeration (like custard), you don't have to put them in the fridge. My recommendation: leave them out and eat them fast!

> Oils: Oils will thicken up and get cloudy in the fridge, though this goes away when you take them out. Except for nut oils (which must be refrigerated), you don't need to refrigerate them, though.

> Apples: Apples are good for about a week stored at room temperature, but you can store them in the fridge for longer. All that matters here is how fast you eat them and whether you like cold apples.

THINGS YOU SHOULD ALWAYS REFRIGERATE

> Meat: This is a no-brainer. Meat will go bad if you don't refrigerate it. Fresh beef (or packaged meat, after opening) should be eaten within 3-5 days; ground meat and fish within 1-2 days.

> Milk: Also reasonably obvious. Store it until about a week after the stamped "sell by" date, then pitch it if you haven't finished it. We've talked about this once before, too, so check out our post on the subject for more info.

> Eggs: This can actually vary a bit—Chow.com notes that certain organic eggs can be left out for a few days—but in general, it's highly recommended to keep all your eggs in the fridge. The last thing you want is a bad egg. For recipes that require eggs at room temperature, just leave them out for 10 minutes before using them.

> Cheese: Unless it comes in a spray can, refrigerate it. Most cheeses recommend you take them out of the fridge for a half hour or so before serving, for optimal texture.

> Condiments, Jams, and Salad Dressings: Basically anything that says "refrigerate after opening" on the bottle. You can store these in the

pantry before you open them (yes, even mayonnaise), but once you open them, stick them in the fridge. The maple mentioned above syrup would fall into this category.

> Butter: This is a hotly contested one. The USDA guidelines recommend freezing it if you aren't going to use it within 1-2 days, and refrigerating all soon-to-be-eaten butter. It says you can leave it out for 10 to 15 minutes for enhanced spreadability (though we've got our tricks for that, too). That said, many people store their butter at room temperature, in a covered dish. Because it's made from pasteurized milk, it's less likely to grow bacteria. This one's really up to you—if you'd rather be safe than sorry, throw it in the fridge, but I and many others find that storing it at room temperature—as long as its properly covered—is okay.

BUYING FRESH AND LOCAL

Depending on where you live, you may have access to locally sourced produce. Local markets are great because you will find the freshest produce and you'll be helping your local economy as well! And if you buy local items when they're in season, you'll probably spend less money than you would at a grocery store. Now isn't that a win-win!?

STOCKING

A well-stocked pantry eliminates the stress out of meal planning and prep because it helps you have the tools you need to produce an incredible meal even if you are too busy to get to the store. This list covers all the nonperishable items you need to make any recipe in this book. Exceeding the basics, it includes healthy convenience items that can help you get nutrition and lots of flavor effortlessly.

OILS AND VINEGARS

- Canola oil
- Cooking spray
- Extra-virgin olive oil Toasted sesame oil Balsamic vinegar Cider vinegar
- Red wine vinegar Rice vinegar

- White wine vinegar

CONDIMENTS, SAUCES, AND OTHER FLAV

- Asian fish sauce Capers
- Chipotle chiles in adobo sauce Cocoa powder, unsweetened, natural Hot pepper sauce
- Instant espresso
- Jarred sauces (basil pesto, marinara, salsa) Jarred roasted red peppers, in water Liquid smoke
- Mayonnaise
- Mustard (grainy, Dijon) Olives (green, Calamata) Porcini mushrooms, dried Soy sauce, low-sodium
- Sun-dried tomatoes, not oil-packed Thai red curry paste Worcestershire sauce
- Wine (dry red, dry white, sparkling, mirin)

On The Shelf

- Applesauce, natural, unsweetened Baking powder
- Baking soda
- Beans, canned, preferably low-sodium (black, cannellini, and navy beans; chickpeas)
- Broth, low-sodium (chicken, beef, vegetable) Chunk light tuna, packed in water
- Chocolate (60% to 70% cocoa solids or bittersweet) Coconut milk, unsweetened, light
- Condensed milk, sweetened, fat-free Evaporated milk
- Gelatin Hominy
- Jams and preserves (apricot, raspberry) Pineapple, packed in natural juice Pumpkin, solid packed
- Salmon, canned
- Tomatoes, preferably no salt added Guice, diced, whole, tomato sauce, tomato paste)

Sweeteners

- Honey
- Pure maple syrup
- Sugar (granulated, brown [light and dark], turbinado, superfine, confectioners')
- Unsulfured molasses

NUTS, SEEDS, AND DRIED FRUITS

- Peanut butter, natural-style (chunky and creamy) Tahini (sesame paste)
- Variety of shelled, unsalted nuts and seeds (almonds, hazelnuts, peanuts, pecans, pine nuts, pistachios, pumpkin seeds, sesame seeds, sunflower seeds, walnuts)
- Dried fruit (apricots, cherries, cranberries, dates, figs, crystallized ginger, raisins)

GRAINS

- Bread crumbs, unseasoned, preferably whole-wheat
- Breakfast cereals (crispy brown rice, Shredded Wheat, All-Bran) Bulgur wheat
- Cornmeal, yellow
- Corn tortilla chips, baked Couscous, whole wheat
- Flour (whole-wheat, whole-wheat pastry, all-purpose) Oats, old-fashioned rolled and quick-cooking
- Pasta (whole-wheat or whole-wheat blend, in a variety of shapes) Pre-cooked rice pouches, microwaveable
- Quinoa
- Rice (white, brown, wild, Arborio) Soba noodles
- Vanilla wafer cookies Wheat berries
- Wheat germ
- Whole-grain graham crackers

IN THE FREEZER

- Broccoli
- Bread (whole-wheat baguettes, sliced bread, pita, buns) Corn kernels
- Edamame, shelled
- Fruit, unsweetened (sliced peaches, mangos, berries, cherries) Ice cream (light) or frozen yogurt, vanilla
- Lima beans Peas
- Ravioli, cheese

SHRIMP

- Spinach, chopped Sorbet, raspberry Tortellini
- Winter squash, pureed Wonton wrappers

THE SPICE RACK

- Almond extract Caraway seeds Cayenne pepper Chili powder
- Crushed red pepper flakes Curry powder
- Dried basil Dried dill Dried oregano Dried thyme
- Ground cinnamon Ground coriander Ground cumin Ground ginger Ground nutmeg Ground oregano Herbes de Provence Peppercorns, black Saffron
- Salt Turmeric
- Vanilla extract

WHICH FRUITS AND VEGETABLES?

While most fruits and vegetables can and should be stored in the fridge, it's a bit more complicated than that. We could probably do a whole Ask Lifehacker on fruits and veggies alone. We've listed some of the more popular fruits in the lists above, but for a more comprehensive list, check out this article at SparkPeople. Not only do they have a handy table of what you should and shouldn't store in the refrigerator, but they highlight how you should store them and which fruits should be kept away from others due to Ethylene—the gas that causes other fruits to over-ripen. We've also talked about this a little before, so check out our article on the subject to brush up on your refrigeration skills.

This isn't a completely comprehensive list, but it should answer some of your questions. You'll see the rules can pretty easily be bent for a lot of foods, so it's up to you how you store them but this should at least keep you informed of the pros and cons of doing so for each food.

FOOD TO EAT EACH SEASON

Eating seasonally not only keeps your wallet full, it also makes eating interesting and fresh. Being separated from the earth, and living far away from farms can make you oblivious to when certain foods are in season, or when they are most abundant in the country. To solve this issue, you can simply go to your local farmer's market, and ask the farmer, or you can keep a list handy like this post. Read on to discover which foods you should be eating now while they last.

WINTER

A lot cooler than fall, winter is the time for exclusively warm foods with warm spices to compliment it. Staying warm is the most paramount item on your list during this time, so choose foods that help out! You might not think fresh foods are available this time of year, but you'd be surprised just how many nutritious ingredients are abundant during the cooler months.

Choose:

- Nuts - In addition to healthy fats and vitamin E, a quarter-cup of nuts, specifically almonds, contains 62 mg of magnesium plus 162 mg of potassium. Winter is the best time to go nuts on nuts, whether you crack them yourself with your grandma's favorite nut cracker, or if you buy them already shelled. Once you have your hands on some, make this fabulous nut cheese, these raw brownies, Vanilla Cashew Maple Butter, or this kick butt gluten free stuffing.

- Brussels Sprouts - Brussels sprouts have a superb glucosinolate content which are important phytonutrients for health because they are the chemical starting points for a variety of cancer-protective substances. The alien heads are back to make your holidays and snow days even better than they already are, so stuff them in a soup, in a nice bake with a maple mustard glaze, or in your favorite gnocchi dish.

- Dates - Dates are wicked awesome, and if you don't already know just how awesome they are, check out this article. Who doesn't love these maple tasting balls of sweet yumminess? Put them in anything from oat squares to marbella to yogi balls, they are always marvelous.

- Turnips - Glucosinolates, sulfur-containing compounds that may reduce the risk of some forms of cancer while providing antifungal, antibacterial and antiparasitic benefits, are an essential part of turnips. The Puritans love them, but they're not a good judge of things, so try them yourself in this ravioli, fry form, or in a club with caramelized onions and toasted lentils.

- Oranges - The vitamin C in oranges is a primary water-soluble antioxidant in the body, disarming free radicals and preventing damage in the aqueous environment both inside and outside cells. The citrus that you find at the bottom of your stocking or growing on trees that smell beautiful are considered a delicacy in the winter, but they are in season in some states. Put them in a chocolate cheesecake, orange cauliflower, cupcakes, or in some French inspired crepes. Essentially, eating seasonally helps to diversify your diet, giving you new things to  eat. This diversity is the foundation of a healthy diet, supplying the body with different nutrients to help it along during the different parts of the year. Whichever season you're in, try and center your diet accordingly.

SPRING

This season is the time of greening in which leafy vegetables and fresh herbs are plentiful. The following pieces of produce should be on your plate in the spring:

- Swiss Chard - Swiss chard, the springtime fairy of green leaves, is rich in vitamin K, A, and C that assists with bone, skin, and teeth rejuvenation. Try this quiche, sauté, or check out how to use it in on five unique ways to eat this amazing leafy green.

- Spinach - What kind of man is Popeye? Well, he's a sailor man, but he's also a spinach man, and for good reason: spinach is rich in vitamins, minerals, health-promoting phytonutrients such as carotenoids (beta-carotene, lutein, and zeaxanthin), and flavonoids which give you a hefty dose of antioxidants.Make some amazing stuffed mushrooms, spinach dip, or a creamy lasagna.

- Romaine Lettuce - Lettuce is scrumdiliumptious, low in calories, high in fiber to keep you regular, and brimming with vitamin C and beta-carotene. Try this green smoothie while you check out why lettuce actually rocks, and then whip up this amazing vegan caesar salad.

- Parsley - Parsley is full of flavonoids—especially luteolin—which function as antioxidants to combine with highly reactive oxygen-containing molecules, helping to prevent oxygen-based damage to cells. Make this wicked squash parsley dip and this parsley enhanced smoothie. For a savory twist, cook up this pasta dish!

- Basil - Basil is a rich source of magnesium which helps to protect the heart by relaxing the surrounding vessels. Noodle and bean salad is so much better with basil, and so is stuffed mushrooms. While you're cooking up a storm with your best friend basil, try out this spaghetti squash and basil dish!

SUMMER

This season, hot and humid, makes you crave cooling foods that are ice cold on your tongue. Light fruits and vegetables are abundant in this season, and so you should indulge in all the berries, melons, and "salad" vegetables like zucchini, cucumbers, and celery.

Enjoy these:

- Strawberries - Strawberries are ideal for the eyes, anti-aging, memory, bone and cardiovascular health. This article has a whopping 25 recipes that all feature the lovely heart berry, but you can also just have a simple chocolate covered strawberry or maybe a strawberry loaf! The possibilities are limitless.

- Summer Squash - As an excellent source of manganese and a very good source of vitamin C, summer squash provides a great combination of antioxidants, but it's carotenoids, lutein and zeaxanthin, are especially important for proper eye function. Never had summer squash, or just need a refresher on how to cook with it? We'll show you how! Or, you can stuff some squash in your breakfast scramble or couscous.

- Watermelon - Watermelon is a high-lycopene food which means that it helps with cardiovascular health and bone health. Summer watermelon is always the best, so why wouldn't you have some with every meal (or at least until you get sick of it). Try it in a salad, smoothie, or a chilled soup.

- Pear - Pears, rich in dietary fiber, help protect against the development of type 2 diabetes (or DM2, which stands for "diabetes mellitus type 2") as well heart disease. Pears are sweet, soft, rich in fiber, and delicious whether you have them in a cocktail, a pie, or a beet smoothie.

- ✓ Broccoli - Broccoli has incredible anti-inflammatory and antioxidant benefits, and it's also a potent source of vitamin C. A vegetable that looks like a little tree has to be delicious, right? Well, if you cook it up in a delicious way, say in this stir fry, salad, or raw soup, then yes, absolutely.

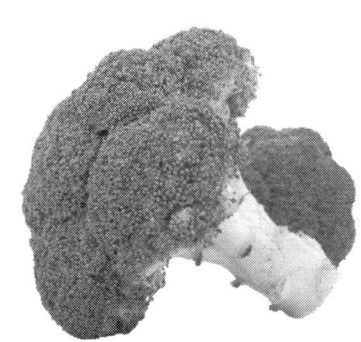

FALL

Rolling in with orange leaves, pumpkin flavors, and smells of cinnamon, fall is the most diverse of seasons, with different types of roots in season, and spices, all constituting as cooling and warming foods.

Here's what to eat as the air turns back cool:

- Carrot - Carrots are super rich in carotenoids to prevent oxidative damage inside the body. Rabbit from Winnie the Pooh can't live without his carrots, and you shouldn't have to either. Make some muffins to kick off the turning of the leaves, or a gluten free cake. Alternatively, you can indulge your savory taste buds with some raw carrot sushi.

- Sweet Potato - With a sizable amount of vitamin A, these starchy tubers make everything healthier and tastier, so why not have some sweet potato and kale patties for dinner and some s'mores sweet potato brownies for dessert? If you're just looking for a light meal, have a sweet potato pie smoothie!

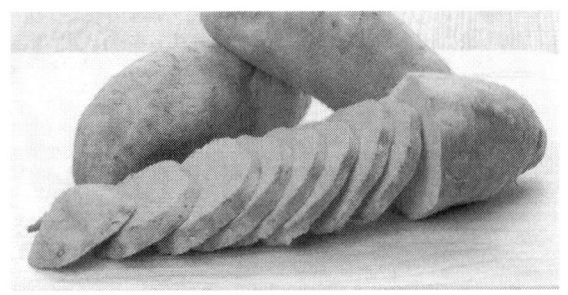

- Onions - Onions provide protection for the heart and blood vessels when consumed in a diet that is rich in other vegetables and fruits—especially flavonoid-containing vegetables and fruits. They're so good they make you cry: onions make everything extra luscious and savory, so throw 'em in a stew, soup, or even a kugel.

- Garlic - Since Halloween is smack dab at the end of fall, you can most definitely use it's potent powers to ward off vampires and amp up the flavors of any dish (well except breakfast porridge). Try this fry up, sweet potato dish, or this tagliatelle pasta pronto before the vampires attack!

- Ginger - This amazing root is rich in sulfur-containing compounds that are responsible for their pungent odors and for many of their health-promoting effects. Your favorite spicy root doesn't just enhance your chai tea, it also produces amazing food products: check out these 10 amazing recipes, or put some pancakes on the grill and top them with this cranberry, pear, ginger sauce.

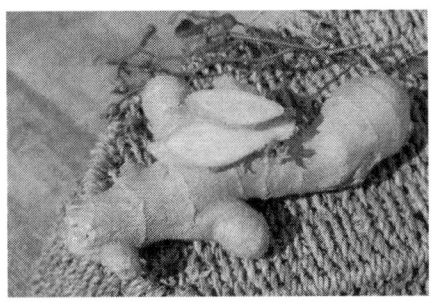

Eating seasonally isn't only beneficial for your wallet and the planet, but it benefits your health (and your taste buds) all the way around. Plants taste so much better when eaten in the season they're grown in. Strive to eat more seasonal foods as the new year approaches and see how your body responds!

CONVERSION TABLE

Oven Temperatures

FAHREINHEIT [F]	CELSIUS [C]
250 °F	120 °C
300 °F	150 °C
325 °F	165 °C
350 °F	180 °C
375 °F	190 °C
400 °F	200 °C
425 °F	220 °C
450 °F	230 °C

Volume Equivalents – "Liquid"

US STANDARD	US STANDARD (OUNCES)	METRIC
2 TABLESPOONS	1 FL. OZ.	30ml
1/4 CUP	2 FL. OZ.	60ml
1/2 CUP	4 FL. OZ.	120ml
1 CUP	8 FL. OZ.	240ml
1-1/2 CUPS	12 FL. OZ.	355ml
2 CUPS	16 FL. OZ.	475ml
4 CUPS	32 FL. OZ.	1 L
1 GALLON	128 FL. OZ.	4 L

Volume Equivalents – "Dry"

US STANDARD	METRIC
1/8 TEASPOON	0.5 ml
1/4 TEASPOON	1ml
1/2 TEASPOON	2ml
3/4 TEASPOON	4ml
1 TEASPOON	5ml
1 TABLESPOON	15ml
1/4 CUP	59ml
1/3 CUP	79ml
1/2 CUP	118ml
2/3 CUP	156ml
3/4 CUP	177ml
1 CUP	235ml
2 CUPS OR 1 PINT	475ml
3 CUPS	700ml
4 CUPS OR 1 QUART	1L
1/2 GALLON	2 L

Weight Equivalents

US STANDARD	METRIC
1/2 OUNCE	15gr
1 OUNCE	30gr
2 OUNCE	60gr
4 OUNCE	115gr
8 OUNCE	225gr
12 OUNCE	340gr
16 OUNCE OR 1 POUND	455gr

BREAKFAST

Raise your hand if breakfast usually means scarfing down a bowl of cereal before rushing out the door. Or a donut off that tray in the office's common room. Or even just a hastily slurped cup of coffee at your desk. Yup, we feel ya.

It's ironic that the meal once known as the "most important" of the day is also the one that most of us have little time for. That's where meal-prepping comes in handy—to make sure you've got good, healthy eats on hand every morning. But we're taking make-ahead breakfast recipes one step further with this roundup and offering you breakfasts that aren't just easy to assemble ahead of time, they're also portable. It doesn't matter if you accidentally overslept or if an early meeting forces you to skip your bagel run, these healthy breakfast ideas guarantee you get your morning fuel.

The recipes in this chapter solve that conundrum. Each and every breakfast here is one you can make in advance to grab and go or whip up in minutes in the morning.

PERFECT-START SMOOTHIE

This ultra-satisfying smoothie is the perfect morning jump start. The fruit and honey hit the sweet spot, and almonds and wheat germ make i nutty and substantial. Pour it in a to-go cup so you can drink it as you dash out the door.

- 1 ripe banana, cut into chunks, frozen
- 6 medium (5 ounces) strawberries, fresh or thawed frozen ones
- 2 cups nonfat milk
- ¼ cup wheat germ
- ¼ cup unsalted almonds
- 2 tablespoons honey
- ½ teaspoon vanilla extract
- 1 cup ice water

Combine all of the ingredients in a blender and blend on high until smooth.

Makes 2 servings

Serving Size

2 ½ cups

Per Serving

Calories 417

Total Fat 10 g

Sat Fat 2 g Mono Fat 6 g Poly Fat 2 g

Protein 15 g

Carb 62 g

Fiber 7 g

Cholesterol 6 mg

Sodium 133 mg

Excellent Source of Calcium, Fiber, Folate, Iodine, Magnesium, Manganese, Phosphorus, Potassium, Protein, Thiamin, Riboflavin, Vitamin C, Zinc

Good Source of Copper, Iron, Pantothenic Acid, Vitamin B6, Vitamin B12

Tip:

Frozen fruit like strawberries is no compromise; it is actually one of the secrets to an extra-cool and frothy smoothie. Besides, it's handy and economical and has comparable nutrition to fresh. Just be sure to buy it unsweetened so you are in control of how much sweetener is added.

Don't toss your overripe bananas. Cut them into chunks and freeze them in plastic bags. Their natural sweetness is perfect in smoothies, and sometimes it's all the sweetener you need.

PEACH SMOOTHIE

Peach for breakfast? Sure, especially when it is in the form of this luscious smoothie.

- 1 cup nonfat milk
- 1 cup nonfat or low-fat vanilla yogurt
- 2 cups frozen sliced peaches (unsweetened)
- 1 tablespoon honey, plus more to taste
- ½ teaspoon vanilla extract
- 1/8 teaspoon ground cinnamon
- Pinch of ground nutmeg
- Pinch of ground ginger
- 1 cup ice

Put all of the ingredients in a blender and blend on high until smooth.

Makes 2 servings

Serving Size

2 cups

Per Serving

Calories 240

Total Fat 0 g

Sat Fat 0 g Mono Fat 0 g Poly Fat 0 g

Protein 14 g

Carb 57 g

Fiber 5 g

Cholesterol 5 mg

Sodium 150 mg

Excellent Source of Calcium, Protein, Vitamin C

Good Source of Fiber, Iodine, Phosphorus, Riboflavin, Vitamin A

CEREZA WITH VANILLA - SMOOTHIE

Cherry and vanilla form an all-American combo that never goes out of style. It really works in this thick, creamy shake that's candy pink and scented with vanilla. One sip and you'll feel like a kid again.

- 2 cups pitted sweet cherries (unsweetened), frozen
- 1 cup nonfat or low-fat vanilla yogurt
- 1 cup nonfat milk
- 2 teaspoons honey
- ½ teaspoon vanilla extract
- 1 cup ice

Combine all of the ingredients in a blender and blend on high until smooth.

Makes 2 servings

Serving Size

2 ½ cups

Per Serving

Calories 280

Total Fat 0 g

Sat Fat 0 g Mono Fat 0 g Poly Fat 0 g

Protein 15 g

Carb 58 g

Fiber 4 g

Cholesterol 6 mg

Sodium 155 mg

Excellent Source of Calcium, Protein, Vitamin C

Good Source of Fiber, iodine, Phosphorus, Riboflavin

ESPRESSO SMOOTHIE

This decedent smoothie does double duty: it's your morning coffee and a filling breakfast, all in one frothy glass. Not to mention that it's a nice chocolate fix. What a way to rev up the day!

- 1 tablespoon sugar
- 2 rounded teaspoons instant espresso, or 2 shots of espresso
- 2 teaspoons unsweetened natural cocoa powder
- ¼ cup boiling water
- 2 cups nonfat milk
- 2 ripe bananas, peeled, cut into chunks, frozen
- 1 cup ice

In a small bowl, stir together the sugar, instant espresso, if using, and cocoa powder. Add the boiling water and stir until dissolved. (If using regular espresso, stir the sugar and cocoa into the coffee until dissolved.)

Combine the coffee mixture in a blender with the milk, bananas, and ice, and blend on high until smooth.

Makes 2 servings

Serving Size

2 ½ cups

Per Serving

Calories 210

Total Fat 1 g

Sat Fat 0.5 g Mono Fat 0.5 g Poly Fat 0 g

Protein 13 g

Carb 47 g

Fiber 45g

Cholesterol 4 mg

Sodium 120 mg

Excellent Source of Calcium, Iodine, Phosphorus, Potassium, Protein, Riboflavin, Vitamin B6, Vitamin C.

Good Source of Fiber, Magnesium, Manganese, Pantothenic Acid, Vitamin B12.

Tip:

To help your morning go more smoothly, put all the smoothie ingredients, except the frozen bananas and ice, in the blender jug the night before. Cover and stash in the refrigerator. In the morning just add the frozen ingredients and whir.

CHESSE-FRUIT TORTILLA

The combination of sharp, rich cheddar with sweet tart apples always wins me over. It's classic yet somehow unique, especially when grilled up in a flour tortilla, so the cheese melts and the apple softens slightly. This takes less than 5 minutes to whip up and will leave you feeling great all morning.

- 1 Granny Smith apple, cored, thinly sliced
- 4 whole-wheat flour tortillas (9 inches in diameter)
- 1 cup shredded sharp cheddar cheese (4 ounces)
- Preheat a large nonstick skillet over medium-high heat.

Fan out the apple slices over the bottom half of each tortilla and top with the cheddar cheese. Fold the tortillas in half. Working in batches, place the quesadillas in the skillet and weigh them down with a smaller heavy skillet or an ovenproof plate topped with a heavy can. Cook until the cheese is melted and the tortillas are golden brown, about 1 ½ minutes per side. Cut in half and eat warm.

Makes 4 servings

Serving Size

1   tortilla

Per Serving

Calories 290

Total Fat 12 g

Sat Fat 6 g Mono Fat 5 g Poly Fat 0 g

Protein 13 g

Carb 31g

Fiber 4 g

Cholesterol 22 mg

Sodium 370 mg

Excellent Source of Calcium, Protein.

Good Source of Fiber, Phosphorus.

SEA FRUITS SANDWICH

This simple sandwich is a remarkably luxurious combination of tastes and textures-buttery smoked salmon, the cool crunch of cucumber, peppery radish, and a whisper of onion from fresh chives-all perfectly packaged between two slices of cream cheese-slathered pumpernickel. Make it the night before and stash it in the fridge for the morning rush.

- ¼ cup whipped cream cheese
- 8 slices pumpernickel bread
- 4 ounces sliced smoked salmon (or another fish)
- 1/8 English cucumber, thinly sliced
- 4 radishes, thinly sliced
- ¼ teaspoon salt
- ¼ teaspoon freshly ground black pepper
- 4 large or 8 small chives

Spread ½ tablespoon of the cream cheese on each slice of the bread. Top four of the bread slices with the salmon, then add the cucumber and radish slices and season with the salt and pepper. Fold 1 large chive or use 2 small chives and place on top. Cover with the remaining slices of bread. Cut each sandwich in half. Eat immediately or wrap in foil and refrigerate for up to 1 day.

Makes 4 servings

Serving Size

1 sandwich

Per Serving

Calories 330

Total Fat 11 g

Sat Fat 3 g Mono Fat 3 g Poly Fat 2 g

Protein 30 g

Carb 38 g

Fiber 4 g

Cholesterol 45 mg

Sodium 615 mg

Excellent Source of Manganese, Niacin, Phosphorus, Protein, Riboflavin, Selenium, Thiamin, Vitamin B12.

Good Source of Copper, Fiber, Folate, Iron, Magnesium, Pantothenic Acid, Potassium, Vitamin B6.

HELL COMBO SANDWICH

If, like me, you regularly spike your eggs with hot sauce, this one's for you. Chunks of egg, creamy avocado, and fresh crisp veggies are doused in tongue-tingling chili sauce, then tucked neatly into a hand-held wrap. It keeps well overnight so you can make it in advance.

- 8 large eggs
- 4 large red-leaf lettuce leaves
- 4 whole-wheat wrap breads (about 9 inches in diameter)
- 1 avocado, pitted, peeled, sliced
- 1 medium tomato (about 4 ounces), sliced
- 1/8 English cucumber, thinly sliced
- 1 tablespoon prepared Thai chili sauce or hot sauce, divided
- ½ teaspoon salt

- ½ teaspoon freshly ground black pepper

Place the eggs in a 4-quart saucepan. Cover with water, bring to a boil, reduce the heat, and simmer for 9 minutes. Remove from the heat, rinse with cold water, and peel. Remove the yolks from 4 of the eggs and discard the yolks. Slice the remaining egg whites and whole eggs into ¼ -inch slices.

Lay a lettuce leaf over the center of each wrap bread. Top each with the avocado, sliced eggs, tomato, and cucumber. Sprinkle with the chili sauce and season with the salt and pepper. Fold one side of the bread about 2 inches over the filling to form a pocket and roll into a wrap. Eat immediately or cover in foil and store in the refrigerator for up to 1 day.

Makes 4 servings

Serving Size 1 wrap

Per Serving

Calories 390

Total Fat 14 g Sat Fat 3 g Mono Fat 7 g Poly Fat 4 g

Protein 30 g

Carb 48 g

Fiber 13 g

Cholesterol 220 mg

Sodium 890 mg

Excellent Source of Fiber, Folate, Iodine, Manganese, Pantothenic Acid, Phosphorus, Protein, Riboflavin, Selenium, Thiamin, Vitamin A, Vitamin B6, Vitamin K.

Good Source of Copper, Iron, Magnesium, Niacin, Potassium, Vitamin B12, Vitamin C, Zinc.

Tip:

For easy, nutrient-rich, and inexpensive protein at your fingertips, cook up a few hard-boiled eggs and stash them in the fridge, where they will last up to a week.

PEANUT BUTTER AND BANANA MIX

Succulent, sweet dates, a hint of cinnamon, and hearty whole-wheat wrap bread give an exciting, exotic twist to your basic peanut butter sandwich. It's a grown-up sandwich that kids will love too. Put it together the night before so all you have to do in the a.m. is pluck it out of the fridge.

- ½ cup natural-style peanut butter
- 4 whole-wheat wrap breads (about 9 inches in diameter)
- 2 bananas, peeled, sliced
- 4 large pitted dates, chopped
- 1 teaspoon ground cinnamon

Spread 2 tablespoons of the peanut butter on each wrap. Evenly distribute the banana slices and dates among the wraps. Sprinkle with cinnamon. Roll the wraps and seal in aluminum foil for easy eating on the go.

Makes 4 servings

Serving Size 1 wrap

Per Serving

Calories 470

Total Fat 19 g Sat Fat 3.5 g Mono Fat 8 g Poly Fat 4.5 g

Protein 15 g

Carb 63 g

Fiber 7 g

Cholesterol 0 mg

Sodium 320 mg

Excellent Source of Fiber, Manganese, Niacin, Protein, Vitamin B6.

Good Source of Copper, Iron, Magnesium, Phosphorus, Potassium.

AUTUMN SPREAD WITH HONEY

The smell of toasting cinnamon raisin bread somehow reassures me that all is well with the world. Spreading that warm bread with a creamy, honey-sweetened walnut spread, then topping it with slices of fresh fruit drives the point home further. It's a deliciously comforting start to the day. Make the spread up to three days ahead of time and refrigerate it so it's ready when you want it.

- ½ cup walnut pieces
- ½ cup plain Greek-style nonfat yogurt
- 2 teaspoons honey
- 8 slices cinnamon raisin bread
- 1 peach (or apple or pear), pitted (or cored)

Toast the walnuts in a dry skillet over medium-high heat, stirring frequently, until fragrant, 3 to 5 minutes. Allow them to cool slightly, and then chop them finely.

In a small bowl, add the chopped walnuts to the yogurt and honey and stir until well combined. The spread will keep in the refrigerator in an airtight container for up to 3 days. Just stir well before using.

When ready to serve, toast the bread and cut the fruit into ¼-inch slices. Spread about 1 tablespoon of the walnut spread onto each piece of bread. Top each piece with a few slices of fruit. Eat immediately.

Makes 4 servings

Serving Size 2 pieces

Per Serving

Calories 230

Total Fat 9 g Sat Fat 0.5 g Mono Fat 0.5 g Poly Fat 3.5 g

Protein 10 g

Carb 42 g

Fiber 4 g

Cholesterol 0 mg

Sodium 220 mg

Excellent Source of Iron, Protein.

Good Source of Fiber, Manganese.

SWEET PUDDING WITH FRUITS

That pudding is a traditional Swiss breakfast that's a mixture of oats, nuts, and fruit.

The oats soften and plump up, becoming like a pudding as they soak in a vanilla-laced honey and milk mixture. Topped with juicy berries and crunchy almonds, these parfaits are so delicious and satisfying you might just start yodeling. Prepare a batch in to-go cups for a true grab-and-go breakfast that will keep in the refrigerator for a few days, or make them in fancy glasses for company.

- ½ cup unsalted raw almonds
- 1 cup nonfat milk
- 1 cup nonfat plain yogurt
- 1 cup old-fashioned rolled oats
- 2 tablespoons honey
- ¼ teaspoon vanilla extract
- 2 cups mixed berries, fresh or frozen (strawberries hulled and halved)

Toast the almonds in a dry skillet over medium-high heat, stirring frequently, until golden and fragrant, about 3 minutes. Chop them coarsely.

In a medium bowl, stir together the milk, yogurt, oats, honey, and vanilla. Divide the oat mixture evenly among 4 small dishes or parfait glasses. Top each with ½ cup of berries, then 2 tablespoons of the chopped almonds. Cover tightly and refrigerate overnight. The parfaits will keep up to 3 days in the refrigerator.

Makes 4 servings

Serving Size

¾ cup pudding

½ cup berries

2 tablespoons almonds

Per Serving

Calories 350

Total Fat 10 g Sat Fat 1 g Mono Fat 6 g Poly Fat 2 g

Protein 15 g

Carb 43g

Fiber 7 g

Cholesterol 0 mg

Sodium 70 mg

Excellent Source of Calcium, Fiber, Manganese, Protein, Vitamin C.

Good Source of Copper, Iodine, Iron, Magnesium, Phosphorus, Riboflavin.

OATMEAL WITH VANILLA FLAVOUR

Oatmeal fragrant with cinnamon, nutmeg, and vanilla, sweetened with rich brown sugar and juicy raisins, and topped with a buttery crunch of pecans, a bowl of this oatmeal is the very essence of comfort. And it's comforting to know you can have it on the table-or in a to-go hot cup-in less than 10 minutes.

- ½ cup pecans
- 3 ½ cups water
- 2 cups old-fashioned rolled oats
- ½ cup raisins
- ¼ teaspoon salt (optional)
- ¼ teaspoon vanilla extract Pinch of ground nutmeg
- 2 tablespoons firmly packed dark brown sugar, plus more to taste
- 1 cup low-fat milk, or to taste
- 1/8 teaspoon ground cinnamon

Toast the pecans in a dry skillet over medium-high heat, stirring frequently, until golden and fragrant, 3 to 5 minutes. Chop them coarsely.

Combine the water, oats, raisins, and salt, if using, in a medium saucepan. Bring to a boil, reduce the heat to low, and simmer, stirring a few times, until the oats are tender, about 5 minutes.

Remove the pan from the heat and stir in the vanilla and nutmeg. Swirl in the brown sugar and place the oatmeal in serving bowls. Pour

A cup of milk on top of each bowl, sprinkle with the toasted pecans and cinnamon, and serve.

Makes 4 servings

Serving Size 1 1/2 cups

Per Serving

Calories 360

Total Fat 13 g Sat Fat 1 g Mono Fat 5.5 g Poly Fat 3 g

Protein 12 g

Carb 54 g

Fiber 5 g

Cholesterol 4 mg

Sodium 190 mg

Excellent Source of fiber, Manganese, Protein.

Good Source of Calcium, Iron.

BRAN MUFFINS

These moist, tender muffins will erase any memories of the rubbery, leaden low-fat muffins you have had before. One of the secrets is the applesauce, which adds extra tenderness and sweet fruity flavor. The figs lend a deep-flavored, sophisticated touch. It's maximum muffin satisfaction with minimal effort.

Cooking spray

- 1 ½ cups bran cereal, such as All-Bran
- 1 cup low-fat milk
- 1 ½ cups whole-wheat flour 1 tablespoon baking powder
- ½ teaspoon salt
- ¾ cup natural applesauce
- ½ cup honey
- 1/3 cup canola oil
- 2 tablespoons unsulfured molasses

- 1 large egg, beaten to blend
- 1 cup chopped dried figs, plus 3 whole dried figs, thinly sliced

Preheat the oven to 400°F. Coat a 12-capacity muffin pan with cooking spray.

In a large bowl, combine the cereal and milk. Let sit until softened, about 5 minutes. Meanwhile, whisk together the flour, baking powder, and salt in a separate bowl.

Add the applesauce, honey, oil, molasses, and egg to the cereal mixture and stir until combined. Add the flour mixture and stir until just combined. Gently stir in the chopped figs. Spoon the batter into the prepared pan and top each muffin with a fig slice. Tap the pan on the counter a few times to remove any air bubbles.

Bake for about 20 minutes or until a wooden toothpick inserted in the center of a muffin comes out clean. Let cool in the pan on a wire rack for 15 minutes. If necessary, run a knife around the muffins to loosen from the tin. Unmold the muffins and cool completely on a rack.

Makes 12 muffins

Serving Size

1 muffin

Per Serving

Calories 260

Total Fat 8 g Sat Fat 1 g Mono Fat 4 g Poly Fat 2 g

Protein 6 g

Carb 43 g

Fiber 6 g

Cholesterol 20 mg

Sodium 130 mg

Excellent Source of Fiber, Folate, Manganese, Phosphorus, Vitamin B6, Vitamin B12.

Good Source of Calcium, Iron, Magnesium, Niacin, Potassium, Riboflavin, Selenium, Thiamin, Zinc.

Make a batch of these muffins on the weekend, wrap them individually in wax paper, and freeze them in a plastic bag. Take one out the night before to defrost at room temperature for a perfect start to a busy day.

LUXURY BREAKFAST

The recipes here are perfect for easing into a day off. They are impressive and special enough for company-not something you'd make if you had to rush out the door-but they don't take much effort at all, leaving you more time to relax and enjoy.

EGG WITH SURPRISE

This sandwich takes the classic comfort bacon-egg-and-cheese sandwich to new heights. Fluffy herb-spiked eggs, smoky bacon, melting cheddar, and a juicy slice of tomato are all piled onto a crunchy English muffin. It's nice to wake up knowing you are just one pan and ten minutes away from total contentment.

- 4 large eggs
- 4 large egg whites
- ¼ cup minced fresh chives
- ¼ cup minced fresh parsley
  Cooking spray
- 4 ½-inch-thick round slices Canadian bacon
- 4 whole-wheat English muffins
- 4 thin slices sharp cheddar cheese (½ ounce each)
- 1 large beefsteak tomato, sliced into ½-inch-thick slices

Crack the eggs and egg whites into a bowl and whisk. Add the chives and parsley and stir to incorporate.

Spray a large nonstick skillet with cooking spray. Ladle ¼ of the egg mixture into the skillet and cook, omelet style, until the eggs are cooked through, 1 to 2 minutes per side. Slide the omelet onto a plate and cover with foil to keep warm. Repeat with remaining eggs.

In the same skillet, heat the Canadian bacon until warm, 1 to 2 minutes per side. Toast the English muffins. Fold each omelet to fit in an English muffin, then place the omelet on one muffin half. Top with the cheese slice, then the bacon slice, and then a tomato slice. Top with the other muffin half and serve.

Makes 4 servings

Serving Size

1 sandwich

Per Serving

Calories 300

Total Fat 14 g

Sat Fat 5 g Mono Fat 3 g Poly Fat 1 g

Protein 30 g

Carb 32 g

Fiber 6 g

Cholesterol 240 mg

Sodium 920 mg

Excellent Source of Calcium, Fiber, Manganese, Niacin, Phosphorus, Protein, Riboflavin, Selenium, Thiamin, Vitamin A, Vitamin C, Vitamin K.

Good Source of Copper, Folate, Iodine, Iron, Magnesium, Potassium, Vitamin B6, Zinc.

Yolks: More Than They're Cracked Up To Be

If you have been sworn to egg-white omelets, you may be missing out on more than you think. True, egg yolks contain all of an egg's fat (5 grams) and cholesterol (212 mg). That's not so much fat, but it is most of the 300 mg daily cholesterol limit.

But surprisingly, yolks also contain most of the egg's nutrients: lots of protein plus rich amounts of over a dozen vitamins and minerals including hard-to-get vitamins D and B12, iron, zinc, brain-protective choline, and the eye-health antioxidants lutein and zeaxanthin. Not to mention that yolks make your egg dishes sunny yellow, rich, and flavorful.

What's a healthy food lover to do? I say split the difference and get the best of both worlds. You can eat up to one yolk a day without overdoing cholesterol. So when serving eggs, include one whole egg and one or two whites per person.

TURKEY EGG WITH ASPARAGUS

Egg in a Basket is one of those simple pleasures you probably remember from childhood-an over-easy egg cooked inside a hole cut out of a piece of bread. This version builds on that fun basic with an easy yet inspired smoked turkey and asparagus topping. It's still simple and still kid friendly but definitely good enough for company.

- ¾ pound asparagus stalks (about bunch) , woody bottoms removed)
- 4 pieces whole-wheat sandwich bread
- 4 teaspoons butter, melted
  Cooking spray
- 6 ounces sliced smoked turkey, sliced again into thin ribbons
- ¼ teaspoon freshly ground black pepper
- 4 large eggs

Place the asparagus in a steamer basket over a pot of boiling water. Cover and steam until crisp-tender, about 3 minutes. Chop the asparagus into ½ -inch pieces.

Brush both sides of each slice of bread with the melted butter. Using a 3-inch cookie cutter, cut a hole in the center of each slice of bread; reserve the cutouts.

Spray a large nonstick skillet with cooking spray and set over medium-high heat. Cook the turkey slices until they are browned around the edges, about 3 minutes. Add the asparagus and cook until it is heated through, about 2 minutes, then season with the pepper.

Transfer the mixture to a plate and cover with foil to keep warm.

Place 2 of the bread slices and cutouts in the same skillet and crack one egg into the hole of each slice. Cook until the egg whites are set and the bread is toasted on the underside, about 3 minutes. Using a spatula, flip the bread/egg slices and cutouts and cook an additional 1 minute. Transfer the bread/egg pieces to individual plates. Repeat with the remaining bread slices and cutouts. Top each one with ¼ of the turkey-asparagus mixture. Arrange the cutouts on each plate.

Makes 4 servings

Serving Size

1 Egg in a Basket with ½ cup asparagus-turkey topping and 1 bread cutout

Per Serving

Calories 290

Total Fat 12 g

Sat Fat 5 g Mono Fat 1.5 g Poly Fat 0.5 g

Protein 23 g

Carb 26 g

Fiber 5 g

Cholesterol 250 mg

Sodium 630 mg

Excellent Source of Manganese, Protein, Selenium, Vitamin A, Vitamin K.

Good Source of Copper, Fiber, Folate, Iron, Magnesium, Niacin, Phosphorus, Riboflavin, Thiamin.

GRANDE BURRITO

Everything about this breakfast is big-big tastes, big portion, and big satisfaction. The only small thing is the effort you need to make it. This soft flour tortilla stuffed with goodies-savory beans, scrambled eggs, spicy salsa, melting cheese, rich avocado, and tangy sour cream- is just the right size to keep you going all morning without weighing you down.

- 2 teaspoons canola oil
- ½ small red onion, diced (1 cup)
- 1 red bell pepper, seeded and diced
- 1 cup canned black beans, preferably low-sodium, drained and rinsed
- ¼ teaspoon crushed red pepper flakes
- Salt and freshly ground black pepper to taste
- 4 large eggs
- 4 large egg whites
- 1/3 cup (about 1 ½ounces) shredded pepper Jack cheese Cooking spray
- 4 whole-wheat flour tortillas (10 inches in diameter; burrito-size)
- ¼ cup reduced-fat sour cream
- ¼ cup salsa
- 1 large tomato (4 ounces), seeded and diced
- 1 small avocado (4 ounces), pitted, peeled, and cubed

- Hot pepper sauce, to taste

Heat the oil in a large nonstick skillet over medium-high heat. Add the onion and red bell pepper and cook, stirring, until softened, about 5 minutes. Add the black beans and red pepper flakes and cook, stirring occasionally, another 3 minutes. Season with salt and pepper, and then transfer the mixture to a bowl.

Whisk the eggs and egg whites together in a medium-size bowl, then add the cheese. Spray the skillet with cooking spray and reheat it over medium heat. Reduce the heat to low, add the eggs, and scramble until cooked through, about 3 minutes.

Spread each tortilla with 1 tablespoon each of sour cream and salsa, then layer with ¼ of the black bean mixture, ¼ of the scrambled eggs, some diced tomato, and ¼ of the avocado. Season to taste with the hot pepper sauce. Roll up burrito-style.

Makes 4 servings

Serving Size

1 burrito

Per Serving

Calories 480

Total Fat 20 g

Sat Fat 6 g Mono Fat 4 g Poly Fat 1 g

Protein 25 g

Carb 53 g

Fiber 13 g

Cholesterol 240 mg

Sodium 860 mg

Excellent Source of Fiber, Protein, Vitamin A, Vitamin C .

Good Source of Calcium, Folate, Iodine, Iron, Potassium, Riboflavin, Selenium, Vitamin B6, Vitamin K.

GRILLED PORTOBELLO MUSHROOMS

Here's a fresh take on a classic Portobello Mushrooms. The base is a savory, juicy grilled portobello mushroom that's layered with Canadian bacon and eggs, then topped with a rich pesto sauce, aromatic basil leaves, and a sprinkle of Parmesan. The taste of each layer amplifies the others for maximum flavor impact.

- Cooking spray
- 4 portobello mushroom caps (about 4 ounces each)
- 1 tablespoon olive oil
- ¼ teaspoon salt, plus more to taste
- 4 slices Canadian bacon
- 4 large eggs
- 4 large egg whites
- 2 tablespoons water
- Freshly ground black pepper to taste
- 4 teaspoons store-bought basil pesto
- 8 fresh basil leaves, cut into ribbons
- 4 teaspoons freshly grated Parmesan cheese
- Preheat a grill or grill pan sprayed with cooking spray.

With a spoon, gently scrape out the dark inside of the mushroom caps (the gills), being careful not to break the cap. Brush both sides of the mushroom caps with oil and sprinkle with ¼ teaspoon of salt. Grill the mushrooms over medium-high heat until they are tender and their juices begin to release, about 7 minutes per side. Transfer each mushroom to a plate, top side down.

On the same grill pan or grill, cook the Canadian bacon slices over medium-high heat until they are warm and grill marks have formed, about 30 seconds per side. Place 1 slice of bacon in each of the mushroom caps.

In a medium-size bowl, whisk the eggs, egg whites, and water together until well combined. Spray a medium-size nonstick skillet with cooking spray and heat over medium-low heat. Add the eggs and scramble until cooked through, about 3 minutes. Season with salt and pepper.

Spoon ¼ of the scrambled eggs on top of the Canadian bacon in each of the mushroom caps. Drizzle 1 teaspoon of pesto over each and top each with some basil ribbons and 1 teaspoon of Parmesan cheese.

Makes 4 servings

Serving Size

1 assembled mushroom cap

Per Serving

Calories 270

Total Fat 15 g

Sat Fat 3.5 g, Mono Fat 5 g, Poly Fat 1 g

Protein 22 g

Carb 7 g

Fiber 3 g

Cholesterol 230 mg

Sodium 720 mg

Excellent Source of Copper, Iodine, Niacin, Pantothenic Acid, Potassium, Protein, Riboflavin, Selenium, Thiamin.

Good Source of Folate, Iron, Manganese, Phosphorus, Vitamin B6, Vitamin B12, Zinc.

EGGS WITH SALMON AND GOLDEN ONION

For this native New Yorker, an ideal weekend day includes an indulgent lox (smoked salmon) and bagel breakfast with a cup of strong coffee and a fat Sunday paper. An afternoon nap and a TV football game don't hurt either. This savory scramble of eggs and smoky salmon with golden caramelized onion is a perfect start..

- 4 large eggs
- 4 large egg whites
- 1 teaspoon canola oil
- 1 large onion, thinly sliced (about 3 cups)
- 4 ounces thinly sliced smoked salmon
- ½ teaspoons cracked black pepper
- ¼ cup thinly sliced chives
- Beefsteak tomato slices

In a medium bowl, whisk the eggs and egg whites. Heat the oil in a large nonstick skillet over medium-high heat. Add the onions and cook, stirring occasionally, until soft and golden brown, 15 to 20 minutes, adding 2 to 3 tablespoons of water after the first 10 minutes to keep the onions moistened. Reduce the heat to medium and add the eggs, smoked salmon, and pepper. Cook, stirring, until the eggs are set, about 5 minutes. Stir in the chives.

Makes 4 servings `

Serving Size

¾ cup egg mixture 2 slices Pumpernickel Crisps and 1 thick tomato slice

Per Serving

Calories 390

Total Fat 10 g

Sat Fat 2.5 g Mono Fat 2 g Poly Fat 1.5 g

Protein 35 g

Carb 38 g

Fiber 3 g

Cholesterol 260 mg

Sodium 420 mg

Excellent Source of Niacin, Phosphorus, Protein, Riboflavin, Selenium, Thiamin, Vitamin B12, Vitamin D.

Good Source of Fiber, Iodine, Iron, Potassium, Vitamin A, Vitamin B6, Vitamin C, Vitamin K.

PUMPERNICKEL CRISPS

2 pumpernickel bagels

Slice each of the bagels into 4 rounds so you wind up with 8 bagel rounds. Toast the bagel rounds in a toaster until crisp, 7 to 8 minutes.

Makes 4 servings

Serving Size

2 slices

HEALTHY BREAKFAST WITH BROCCOLI

This dish and the Blueberry-Almond French Toast Bake lets you serve something extraordinary for breakfast while keeping your morning totally fuss-free. You whip them up the night before so all you have to do when you wake up is pull the dish out of the refrigerator and bake. They puff up beautifully and golden brown, almost like a soufflé. This bake elevates the crowd-pleasing broccoli-cheddar duo to something glorious.

- 2 teaspoons olive oil
- 1 large onion, diced (about 2 cups) Cooking spray
- 1 whole-wheat baguette (about 18 inches long, 8 ounces), cut into 1-inch cubes
- 8 large eggs
- 8 large egg whites
- 2 cups low-fat (1 ¾) milk
- 1 (10-ounce) package frozen chopped broccoli, thawed
- 1 ½ cups shredded extra-sharp cheddar cheese (6 ounces)
- ¾ teaspoon ground nutmeg
- ½ teaspoon salt
- ½ teaspoon freshly ground black pepper

Heat the oil in a nonstick skillet over medium-high heat. Add the onions and cook, stirring, until translucent and beginning to brown, about 4 minutes. Set aside to cool.

Spray a 9x 13-inch baking dish with cooking spray. Arrange the bread cubes in the dish. In a large bowl, beat the eggs, egg whites, and milk until incorporated. Add the onions, broccoli, cheese, nutmeg, salt, and pepper and stir to incorporate. Pour the egg mixture over the bread, spreading it around so the liquid saturates the bread. Cover with plastic wrap and refrigerate for at least 8 hours or overnight.

Preheat the oven to 350°F. Remove the plastic wrap and bake until the top forms a light brown crust, 50 to 60 minutes. Serve hot.

Makes 8 servings

Serving Size

One 4x3-inch piece

Per Serving

Calories 330

Total Fat 15 g

Sat Fat 8 g Mono Fat 3.5 g Poly Fat 1 g

Protein 23 g

Carb 20 g

Fiber 3 g

Cholesterol 235 mg

Sodium 580 mg

Excellent Source of Calcium, Iodine, Manganese, Phosphorus, Protein, Riboflavin, Selenium, Vitamin C.

Good Source of Fiber, Folate, Magnesium, Pantothenic Acid, Potassium, Thiamin, Vitamin A, Vitamin B6, Vitamin B12, Vitamin D.

SWEET FRENCH TOAST

Special days call for special breakfasts, and nothing does the trick better than chocolate. It instantly turns the morning into a celebration. This decadent French toast seems so sinful, stuffed with creamy cheese and melted chocolate and dusted with sugar. But with whole grain, fruit, and fat-free milk, it definitely gets a nod from this nutritionist.

- ¼ cups nonfat milk
- 3 large eggs
- ½ teaspoon vanilla extract
- ¼ cup part-skim ricotta cheese
- 8 slices whole-wheat sandwich bread, crusts removed
- 1 (8-ounce) container fresh strawberries, hulled and sliced
- 4 teaspoons bittersweet chocolate chips
- Cooking spray
- 2 teaspoons confectioners' sugar

In a large bowl, whisk together the milk, eggs, and vanilla. Set aside.

Place 1 tablespoon of the ricotta cheese in the center of 4 of the slices of bread and spread around slightly. Top each with about 6 slices of strawberries and 1 teaspoon of chocolate chips. Cover each with another piece of bread to make a "sandwich."

Spray a large nonstick skillet or griddle with cooking spray and preheat over medium heat. Carefully dip each of the "sandwiches" into the egg mixture until completely moistened. Then place on the skillet and cook until the outside is golden brown, the center is warm and the chocolate is melted, 3 to 4 minutes per side.

Transfer to serving dishes. Top with the remaining strawberries and sprinkle with the confectioners' sugar.

Makes 4 servings

Serving Size

1 "sandwich"

Per Serving

Calories 290

Total Fat 8 g

Sat Fat 3 g Mono Fat 2 g Poly Fat 0 g

Protein 16 g

Carb 39 g

Fiber 5 g

Cholesterol 165 mg

Sodium 390 mg

Excellent Source of Fiber, Iodine, Phosphorus, Protein, Riboflavin, Selenium, Vitamin C.

Good Source of Calcium, Iron, Manganese, Thiamin, Vitamin B12.

TASTY FRENCH TOAST BAKE

The hardest thing about this dish is waiting for it to come out of the oven, because as it is baking it fills your kitchen with the most enticing, heartwarming, vanilla-cinnamon aroma. Its looks and taste hold up their end of the bargain too. Inside, it is eggy, perfectly sweetened, and studded with bursting warm blueberries. Outside, it is crisp and crowned with sugared toasted almonds.

Cooking spray

- 1 whole-wheat baguette (about 18 inches long, 8 ounces), cut into 1-inch cubes
- 2 cups low-fat (1 %) milk
- 8 large eggs
- 8 large egg whites
- 1/3 cup pure maple syrup 1 teaspoon vanilla extract
- ½ teaspoon ground cinnamon 2 cups fresh blueberries
- 1/3 cup sliced almonds
- 2 tablespoons dark brown sugar

Spray a 9x13-inch baking pan with cooking spray. Arrange the bread in a single layer in the baking pan. Whisk together the milk, eggs, egg whites, maple syrup, vanilla, and cinnamon. Pour the egg mixture over the bread in the pan, spreading it around so the liquid saturates the bread. Scatter the blueberries evenly on top. Sprinkle with the almonds and brown sugar.

Cover and refrigerate for at least 8 hours or overnight.

Preheat the oven to 350°F. Uncover and bake for 50 to 60 minutes. Serve hot.

Makes 8 servings

Serving Size

1 4x3-inch piece

Per Serving

Calories 270

Total Fat 8 g

Sat Fat 2.5 g Mono Fat 2 g Poly Fat 0.75 g

Protein 16 g

Carb 35 g

Fiber 3 g

Cholesterol 220 mg

Sodium 280 mg

Excellent Source of Iodine, Manganese, Protein, Riboflavin, Selenium.

Good Source of Calcium, Fiber, Iron, Magnesium, Phosphorus, Vitamin K, Zinc.

PANCAKE WITH PEACH

When this pancake comes out of the oven in its dramatic puffed and golden splendor, your guests will think you really went out of your way for them. Let them think that. Only you'll know that all you did was mix a few simple ingredients together and pour them into a skillet.

- ½ cup all-purpose flour
- ½ cup whole-wheat pastry flour or regular whole-wheat flour 4 teaspoons sugar
- ½ teaspoon salt
- 1 cup low-fat (1 %) milk
- 2 large eggs
- 2 large egg whites Grated zest of 1 lemon 4 teaspoons butter

Preheat the oven to 450°F.

In a medium bowl, whisk together the flours, sugar, and salt. In another bowl, whisk the milk, eggs, egg whites, and lemon zest. Add the wet ingredients to the dry ingredients and mix until just combined.

In a heavy 10-inch cast-iron or ovenproofnonstick skillet, heat the butter until very hot but not smoking. Pour the batter into the skillet and quickly transfer it to the oven. Bake for 25 minutes, until golden brown and puffed; do not open oven during baking. Serve immediately with the Peach Compote.

Makes 4 servings

Serving Size

¼ Dutch baby and 1/3 cup Peach Compote

Per Serving

Calories 320

Total Fat 7 g

Sat Fat 3.5 g Mono Fat 1.25 g Poly Fat 0 g

Protein 11 g

Carb 54 g

Fiber 3 g

Cholesterol 120 mg

Sodium 530 mg

Excellent Source of Manganese, Protein, Thiamin.

Good Source of Calcium, Fiber, Iodine, Iron, Niacin, Potassium, Riboflavin, Vitamin A, Vitamin C.

PEACH COMPOTE WITH MAPLE SYRUP

This delightful peachy topping is a perfect accompaniment for the Dutch Baby Pancake. In fact, it's delicious with just about any pancake, French toast, or waffle. It's also fantastic with yogurt or ice cream.

- 3 large ripe peaches or 4 cups (about 15 ounces) unsweetened frozen sliced peaches
- ¼ cup pure maple syrup
- 1 tablespoon fresh lemon juice 1 tablespoon water
- ½ teaspoon ground cinnamon
- ½ teaspoon vanilla extract
- ½ teaspoon salt

If using fresh peaches, bring a 4-quart pot of water to a boil and fill a large bowl with ice water. With a paring knife, slice through each peach skin all the way around the fruit, but leave the peach intact.

Gently place the peaches into the boiling water and boil for 30 seconds. Transfer the peaches into the ice water for 30 seconds, then remove them using a slotted spoon. Gently remove the skins from the peaches, then split the peaches in half and remove the pits. Cut each peach into 8 slices.

Place the peach slices, maple syrup, lemon juice, water, cinnamon, vanilla, and salt in a saucepan and bring to a boil. Reduce the heat and simmer until the mixture has thickened slightly, about 5 minutes. The compote will keep for up to 3 days in an airtight container in the refrigerator.

Makes 4 servings

Serving Size

1/3 cup

Local, Organic, Better.

WHOLE-WHEAT FRUIT PANCAKES WITH NUTTY TOPPING

Pancakes are my daughter Bella's favorite food to make and eat. She knows the recipe for this apple-laced version by heart. The batter lasts in the fridge for up to two days, so we whip up a double batch on a Sunday to have it on hand for the beginning of the week. It sure makes Monday mornings a lot easier to face!

- 1 medium apple (such as Golden Delicious), cored and diced (about 2 cups)
- ¾ cup all-purpose flour
- ¾ cup whole-wheat flour
- 2 teaspoons baking powder
- ½ teaspoon baking soda
- ¼ teaspoon salt
- 1 cup low-fat (1%) buttermilk
- ¾ cup nonfat milk
- 2 large eggs
- 1 tablespoon honey
- 1 recipe Nutty Topping
- 6 tablespoons pure maple syrup, plus more to taste

Put the apple in a microwave-safe bowl, tightly cover with plastic wrap, and microwave on high until softened, about 2 minutes.

In a large bowl, whisk the flours, baking powder, baking soda, and salt. In a small bowl, whisk together the buttermilk, milk, eggs, and honey. Slowly add the egg mixture to the dry ingredients, stirring until just combined.

Heat a large nonstick griddle over medium heat. Spoon about ¼ cup of the batter per pancake onto the griddle and distribute about a heaping tablespoon of the cooked apple on top. Drizzle a little more batter on top to coat the apple. Flip when the pancake tops are covered with bubbles and the edges look cooked, about 2 minutes. Cook until the pancakes are golden brown and cooked through, an additional 1 to 2 minutes. Serve immediately, or transfer the cooked pancakes to an ovenproof dish and keep warm in a 250°F oven while making the rest.

To serve, arrange 2 pancakes on each plate and sprinkle each serving with about 2 heaping tablespoons of the Nutty Topping. Serve with maple syrup.

Makes 6 servings

Serving Size

2 pancakes with topping and 1 tablespoon syrup

Per Serving

Calories 410

Total Fat 12 g

Sat Fat 2.5 g Mono Fat 3 g Poly Fat 2.5 g

Protein 15 g

Carb 63 g

Fiber 6 g

Cholesterol 75 mg

Sodium 450 mg

Excellent Source of Calcium, Fiber, Iron, Magnesium, Manganese, Phosphorus, Protein, Selenium, Zinc.

Good Source of Copper, Folate, Niacin, Potassium, Riboflavin, Thiamin.

ALMONDS TOPPING

The apple pancakes are great on their own, but this ambrosial nutty topping brings them to the next level. The topping is also incredible in hot or cold cereal, stirred into yogurt, with fruit salad, or as a snack on its own. Consider yourself fairly warned, though: it's addictive.

- ¼ cup hulled (green) pumpkin seeds
- ¼ cup sliced almonds
- ¼ cup shelled sunflower seeds
- 1 tablespoon sesame seeds
- ¼ cup toasted wheat germ
- ¼ cup pure maple syrup Salt to taste

In a large skillet, toast the pumpkin seeds and almonds over medium- high heat, stirring, for about 1 minute. Add the sunflower seeds and cook, stirring, for 1 minute more. Add the sesame seeds to the pan.

Cover and cook, shaking the pan, until the seeds are toasted, about 30 seconds more. Transfer the toasted nuts and seeds to a medium-size bowl. Add the wheat germ. Stir in the syrup and season with salt. The topping will keep for a week in an airtight container.

Makes 6 servings

Serving Size

2 heaping tablespoons

HONEY QUINOA

I always thought of quinoa as a savory side dish until my Peruvian friend told me that there they eat it for breakfast cooked with apples and honey. So I tried it, tossing in some chewy dried cranberries and crunchy pecans for good measure, and discovered my new favorite hot breakfast cereal.

- 1 1/3 cups quinoa
- 2 2/3 cups water
- 1 small Golden Delicious apple, cored and cut into chunks
- ¼ cup dried cranberries

- ½ cup pecans
- ½ cup low-fat (1 ¾) milk, plus more for serving
- 2 tablespoons honey, plus more for serving
- ½ teaspoon ground cinnamon
- 4 teaspoons unsalted butter, optional

Put the quinoa in a fine-mesh strainer and rinse under the tap. Put the rinsed quinoa in a saucepan with the water. Bring to a boil, then reduce the heat to a simmer, cover and cook for 5 minutes. Add the apple chunks and cranberries and continue to cook, covered over low heat, until the water is absorbed, about 10 minutes more.

In the meantime, toast the pecans in a dry skillet over medium-high heat, stirring frequently, until fragrant, about 2 minutes. Allow to cool, then coarsely chop.

When the quinoa is cooked, stir in ½ cup of milk, 2 tablespoons of honey, and the cinnamon, and cook until the milk is heated through, about 1 more minute.

Spoon the cereal into serving bowls and top with the toasted pecans and butter, if using. Serve with additional honey and milk to taste.

Makes 4 servings

Serving Size

1 ¼ cups

Per Serving

Calories 370

Total Fat 14 g

Sat Fat 1.5 g Mono Fat 6.5 g Poly Fat 5 g

Protein 12 g

Carb 57 g

Fiber 6 g

Cholesterol 0 mg

Sodium 25 mg

Excellent Source of Copper, Fiber, Folate, Magnesium, Manganese, Protein, Thiamin.

Good Source of Iron, Potassium, Riboflavin, Vitamin B6, Zinc.

LUNCH PACK TO GO

Lunch hour is more like the twenty-minute lunch, it is harder than ever to eat right at midday. In fact, with life's hectic pace, it is easy to forget about lunch altogether. That is until you are about to pass out from hunger at 3 p.m., at which point you grab the first thing you can find-something that's probably not very good or good for you. But there is one sure way to have a fantastic meal whenever and wherever you need it: bring it with you.

Every lunch here is an absolutely delicious, nutritionally balanced, make-ahead, fully travel-tested meal. Forget about that boring turkey sandwich or soggy salads-I am talking about truly inspired, perfectly-packed food that will turn your lunch box into a treasure chest you will look forward to digging into all morning and that will energize your afternoon.

EXOTIC CHICKEN SALAD

This salad is one of my favorites to bring to a party, so it always puts me in a festive mood when I have it for lunch on a work day. With chunks of chicken in a gorgeous yellow, creamy curry sauce, juicy grapes, and crunchy almonds, it somehow manages to be exotic and comfortably familiar at the same time.

- ¼ cup sliced almonds
- ½ cup nonfat plain yogurt
- 2 tablespoons mayonnaise
- 1 teaspoon curry powder
- 2 ½ cups cubed cooked chicken breasts (about 1 ¼ pounds)
- 1 cup halved red grapes
- ¼ cup chopped cilantro
- Salt and freshly ground black pepper to taste
- 5 ounces mixed greens (about 5 cups lightly packed)
- 4 lemon wedges
- 4 ounces pita chips

Toast the almonds in a small dry skillet over medium-high heat, stirring occasionally, until fragrant and beginning to turn golden, 2 to 3 minutes.

In a large bowl, stir together the yogurt, mayonnaise, and curry powder. Fold in the chicken, grapes, and cilantro and season with salt and pepper. This salad will keep in an airtight container in the refrigerator for up to 3 days.

To serve, put a scoop of the chicken salad on a bed of greens on a plate or in a to-go container and sprinkle with the toasted almonds. Add a lemon wedge to squeeze over the greens just before eating. Serve with pita chips, stored in a separate container, if packing.

Makes 4 servings

Serving Size

1 cup chicken salad, 1 ¼ cups mixed greens, 1 lemon wedge, and 1 ounce pita chips

Per Serving

Calories 420

Total Fat 16 g

Sat Fat 2 g Mono Fat 4 g Poly Fat 4.5 g

Protein 39 g

Carb 27 g

Fiber 4 g

Cholesterol 80 mg

Sodium 460 mg

Excellent Source of Niacin, Phosphorus, Protein, Selenium, Vitamin A, Vitamin B6, Vitamin C.

Good Source of Calcium, Fiber, Iron, Magnesium, Manganese, Potassium, Riboflavin..

LEMON-CUMIN GRILLED CHICKEN

This hearty salad is bursting with harvest flavors and chock-full of exciting textures-chewy yet tender wheat berries, sweet-tart dried cherries, crunchy walnuts, and crisp celery. Served over leafy spinach and topped with cumin-scented chicken, this is a power lunch that will fill you up without slowing you down.

- 1 cup hard wheat berries
- ½ cup chopped walnuts
- 2 stalks celery, finely chopped
- 1/3 cup finely chopped parsley
- 1/3 cup tart dried cherries, chopped
- 1 small scallion (white and green parts), chopped
- 2 tablespoons olive oil
- 1 tablespoon plus 1 teaspoon fresh lemonjuice, plus 4 lemon wedges for serving
- Salt and freshly ground black pepper to taste
- 4 cups lightly packed baby spinach leaves
- 1 recipe Lemon-Cumin Grilled Chicken Breast

In a medium-size pot, combine the wheat berries and enough water to come 2 inches above the wheat berries. Bring to a boil, then reduce the heat to a simmer. Cook, uncovered, until tender, about 1 hour.

Drain and let cool.

Meanwhile, toast the walnuts in a medium-size dry skillet over medium-high heat, stirring occasionally, until fragrant, 2 to 3 minutes.

In a large bowl, combine the wheat berries, toasted walnuts, celery, parsley, dried cherries, scallions, olive oil, and lemon juice. Season with salt and pepper. This salad will keep up to 5 days in an airtight container in the refrigerator.

To serve, place 1 cup of spinach leaves on each plate or in to-go containers. Mound ¾ cup of the wheat berry salad on top of each serving and top that with slices of the Lemon-Cumin Grilled Chicken.

Place a lemon wedge on the side of each serving. Right before eating, squeeze the lemon wedges on top.

Makes 4 servings

Serving Size

¾ cup wheat berry salad, 1 cup spinach, and 7 slices chicken

Per Serving

Calories 580

Total Fat 23 g

Sat Fat 3 g Mono Fat 9 g Poly Fat 8.5 g

Protein 41 g

Carb 50 g

Fiber 8 g

Cholesterol 80 mg

Sodium 420 mg

Excellent Source of Fiber, Iron, Manganese, Niacin, Phosphorus, Protein, Selenium, Vitamin A, Vitamin B, Vitamin C, Vitamin K.

Good Source of Copper, Magnesium, Pantothenic Acid, Potassium.

Did You Know?

Studies show that the act of chewing can help relieve stress, so go for a chewy-crunchy lunch, like this wheat berry salad, to help take the edge off midday.

SOURISH CHICKEN BREAST

A touch of aromatic cumin and a citrus punch take basic grilled chicken to the next level.

- 1 ¼ pounds skinless boneless chicken breasts
- 1 teaspoon ground cumin
- ½ teaspoon salt
- ¼ teaspoon freshly ground black pepper
- 2 teaspoons olive oil
- Cooking spray
- 2 tablespoons fresh lemon juice

Put the chicken between 2 pieces of plastic wrap and pound it slightly with a mallet or rolling pin so it is an even thickness of about ½ inch.

In a small bowl, combine the cumin, salt, and pepper. Rub the chicken breasts on both sides with olive oil and then rub the spice mixture on both sides.

Spray a grill or nonstick grill pan with cooking spray and heat over medium-high heat. Grill the chicken until grill marks have formed and the chicken is cooked through, 3 to 4 minutes per side. Remove from the heat, let rest for 5 minutes, then slice into V2-inch-thick slices and drizzle with the lemon juice. The chicken will keep for up to 3 days in an airtight container in the refrigerator.

Makes 4 servings

Serving Size

About 7 slices chicken

POACHED CHICKEN BREAST

- 1 cup low-sodium chicken broth
- 1 cup water
- 1 ¼ pounds skinless boneless chicken breasts

Bring the broth and water to a boil in a medium saucepan. Put the chicken between 2 pieces of plastic wrap and pound it slightly with a mallet or rolling pin so it is an even thickness of about ½ inch. Add the chicken to the broth and simmer, covered, for 8 minutes. Turn the heat off and let chicken stand in the cooking liquid, covered, until cooked through, about 20 minutes. Remove the chicken from the broth and serve or chill.

Makes 4 servings

Per Serving

Calories 150

Total Fat 3.5 g

Sat Fat 1 g Mono Fat 1 g Poly Fat . 75 g

Protein 29 g

Carb 0 g

Fiber 0 g

Cholesterol 80 mg

Sodium 70 mg

Excellent Source of Niacin, Phosphorus, Protein, Selenium, Vitamin B6.

PASTA SALAD

Imagine a decadently rich creamy pasta salad that's actually good for you. Well, here you have it. The secret is in the dressing, which has a base of tangy thickened yogurt that's the ideal foil for the rich salmon. Sweet peas stud the dish with beautiful color, and dill and scallion make it delightfully fragrant and flavorful.

- 2/3 cup plain Greek-style nonfat yogurt 3 tablespoons fresh lemon juice

- 3 tablespoons mayonnaise
- 2 teaspoons finely grated lemon zest
- 1 teaspoon minced fresh dill, or 2 teaspoons dried
- ½ teaspoon salt
- ½ teaspoon freshly ground black pepper
- 1 (14-ounce) can wild red salmon, drained, skinned and boned, and cut into chunks
- 1 (10-ounce) package frozen peas, defrosted
- ½ pound bowtie or corkscrew pasta, cooked according to package directions and cooled
- 2 scallions (white and green parts), minced (about ¼ cup)
- 8 cups chopped red-leaf lettuce

Combine the yogurt, lemon juice, mayonnaise, lemon zest, dill, salt, and pepper in a bowl and whisk to incorporate. Add the salmon, peas, pasta, and scallions and toss to incorporate. The pasta salad will keep up to 2 days in an airtight container in the refrigerator.

To serve, mound 2 cups of the lettuce onto each plate or into to-go containers and scoop about 1 ¾ cups of the pasta salad on top.

Makes 4 servings

Serving Size

1 ¾ cups pasta salad and 2 cups lettuce

Per Serving

Calories 500 g

Total Fat 14 g

Sat Fat 2 g Mono Fat 1.75 g Poly Fat 1.5 g

Protein 37 g

Carb 56 g

Fiber 6 g

Cholesterol 55 mg

Sodium 730 mg

Excellent Source of Fiber, Folate, Iron, Magnesium, Manganese, Niacin, Phosphorus, Protein, Riboflavin, Selenium, Thiamin, Vitamin A, Vitamin B12, Vitamin C, Vitamin D, Vitamin K.

Good Source of Copper, Potassium, Vitamin B6, Zinc.

SALAD A LA NICE

This classic salad from Nice, France, is usually made with tuna, but salmon makes it richer and more luxurious. The zesty lemon Dijon dressing balances that richness perfectly. You can make this any time of the year, but it is especially lovely in the summer when you can get the produce freshly picked from the farm stand.

- ¾ ound red new potatoes, quartered
- ½ pound green beans, trimmed
- 2 (9-ounce) skinless salmon fillets
- ½ teaspoon salt
- ½ teaspoon freshly ground black pepper
- 1 head Boston or Bibb lettuce, leaves separated
- ½ pint grape tomatoes
- 1/3 cup Nicoise, Calamata, or other black olives
- ¼ cup extra-virgin olive oil
- 1 tablespoon plus 1 teaspoon fresh lemon juice
- 1 tablespoon Dijon mustard

Place the potatoes in a steamer basket over a pot of boiling water. Cover and steam for 6 minutes. Add the green beans to the steamer and continue cooking for 4 minutes more. Transfer the potatoes and green beans to a bowl and set aside to cool.

Preheat a grill or grill pan over medium-high heat. Season the salmon with ¼ teaspoon of salt and ¼ teaspoon of pepper. Grill the salmon, turning once, for 3 to 5 minutes per side for medium doneness. Cut each piece of salmon in half crosswise. Set aside to cool.

Make a bed of about 5 lettuce leaves on each serving plate or in to-go serving containers. Top with a piece of the salmon. Divide the green beans, potatoes, tomatoes, and olives among the servings, arranging each vegetable in a separate pile on the plate.

In a small bowl, whisk together the oil, lemon juice, Dijon mustard, and the remaining ¼ teaspoon each of salt and pepper. For lunch on the go, put 2 tablespoons of dressing in a small separate container. Drizzle the salad with dressing right before serving.

Makes 4 servings

Serving Size

4 ounces cooked salmon, 5 lettuce leaves, 10 green beans, ½ cup potatoes, 1 ½ tablespoons olives, and 2 tablespoons dressing

Per Serving

Calories 450

Total Fat 24 g

Sat Fat 3.5 g Mono Fat 13.5 g Poly Fat 5.5 g

Protein 33 g

Carb 26 g

Fiber 7 g

Cholesterol 70 mg

Sodium 510 mg

Excellent Source of Copper, Fiber, Folate, Magnesium, Manganese, Niacin, Pantothenic Acid, Phosphorus, Potassium, Protein, Riboflavin, Selenium, Thiamin, Vitamin A, Vitamin B6, Vitamin B12, Vitamin C, Vitamin D, Vitamin K.

Good Source of Iron, Zinc.

BEEF TACO SALAD WITH TOMATO DRESSING

There's nothing dainty about this salad. With mounds of chili-spiced beef and sharp cheddar cheese over a bed of crisp greens, all doused with a chunky tomato-lime dressing and topped with shards of corn chips, it has high-impact flavor and heartiness to satisfy even the biggest appetites.

For The Meat

- ¾ pound lean ground beef (90% lean or higher)
- 1 (15. 5-ounce) can black beans, preferably low-sodium, drained and rinsed
- 2 cloves garlic, minced
- 1/3 cup water
- 1 tablespoon chili powder
- 1/8 teaspoon cayenne pepper, plus more to taste

For The Dressing

- 4 medium tomatoes, chopped
- 2 tablespoons extra-virgin olive oil
- 2 tablespoons fresh lime juice
- ½ teaspoon salt
- ¼ teaspoon freshly ground black pepper

For The Salad

- 2 hearts of romaine lettuce, chopped
- ½ cup grated cheddar cheese (2 ounces)
- 2 ounces baked corn tortilla chips (about 32 chips)

Heat a large skillet over medium-high heat. Add the beef and cook until no longer pink, breaking up the meat with a spoon. Add the beans and garlic and cook for 2 minutes more. Add the water, chili powder, and cayenne and stir until well combined. Remove from the heat and allow the mixture to cool slightly.

In a medium bowl, combine the tomatoes (with their juices), oil, lime juice, salt, and pepper. The dressing and meat mixture may be prepared up to 2 days ahead and stored in airtight containers in the refrigerator.

To serve, place 2 cups of lettuce on each plate or in lunch containers. Top each serving with 1 cup of the beef mixture, then sprinkle with 2 tablespoons of cheese. If making to go, pack ¾ cup of the chunky tomato dressing in a separate sealable container and put about 8 chips in a separate bag. Right before eating, top each salad with dressing, and crush the tortilla chips on top.

Makes 4 servings

Serving Size

2 cups lettuce, 1 cup beef mixture, 2 tablespoons cheese, ¾ cup chunky tomato dressing, and about 8 crushed tortilla chips

Per Serving

Calories 450

Total Fat 22 g

Sat Fat 8 g Mono Fat 10 g Poly Fat 2 g

Protein 32 g

Carb 37 g

Fiber 10 g

Cholesterol 70 mg

Sodium 770 mg

Excellent Source of Calcium, Fiber, Iron, Niacin, Phosphorus, Potassium, Protein, Selenium, Vitamin A, Vitamin B6, Vitamin B12, Vitamin C, Zinc.

Good Source of Manganese, Riboflavin, Vitamin K.

MULTICOLOR SALAD

This trio of lettuces is an irresistible balance of peppery robust tastes, crisp and tender textures, and beautiful colors. The balsamic vinegar adds just the right sweet acidity to bring it all together and white beans and cheese make it a complete, satisfying meal. It's a whole lot of goodness for very little effort.

- 5 cups lightly packed arugula (about 5 ounces)
- 1 head radicchio, core removed, sliced
- 2 Belgian endives, bottom ½ inch removed, sliced
- 1 (15-ounce) can white beans (such as cannellini; preferably low- sodium) , drained and rinsed
- ½ cup shaved Parmesan cheese (about 2 ounces)
- ¼ cup extra-virgin olive oil
- 2 tablespoons balsamic vinegar
- ½ teaspoon salt
- 8 Italian bread sticks

In a large bowl, toss together the arugula, radicchio, endive, beans, and Parmesan. In a small bowl, whisk together the oil, vinegar, and salt.

To serve, place 3 cups of the salad in a large bowl or lunch container. If preparing a salad to go, put 1½ tablespoons of the dressing into a small container. Toss with the dressing right before eating. Serve with breadsticks on the side.

Makes 4 servings

Serving Size

3 cups salad, 1 1/2 tablespoons dressing, 2 breadsticks

Per Serving

Calories 360 g

Total Fat 21 g

Sat Fat 4 g Mono Fat 10 g Poly Fat 2 g

Protein 17 g

Carb 31 g

Fiber 7 g

Cholesterol 10 mg

Sodium 540 mg

Excellent Source of Calcium, Fiber, Folate, Magnesium, Manganese, Protein, Thiamin, Vitamin A, Vitamin C, Vitamin K.

Good Source of Copper, Iron, Phosphorus, Potassium, Riboflavin, Zinc.

GREEK SALAD WITH CHICKEN AND FETA

Here all the mouthwatering Greek salad essentials are stuffed into portable pita pockets. Be sure to include the fresh mint-it really lights up the sandwich. As a bonus, the lemony feta spread doubles as a dip that's fantastic with cool, crisp veggies, like cucumber, celery, or red bell pepper.

For The Spread

- ¾ cup crumbled feta cheese (4 ounces)
- 3 tablespoons nonfat plain yogurt
- 1 tablespoon fresh lemon juice
- 2 teaspoons dried oregano

- 1 teaspoon finely grated lemon zest
- ¼ teaspoon freshly ground black pepper

For The Sandwich

- 4 whole-wheat pita breads
- 4 large pieces romaine lettuce, torn in half
- 1 English cucumber, sliced into half moons
- ¼ cup lightly packed fresh mint leaves
- ¾ pound thinly sliced roasted chicken breast

In a medium bowl, combine the feta cheese and yogurt with a fork, mashing any large chunks of cheese. Stir in the lemon juice, oregano, lemon zest, and pepper. The spread will keep for up to 5 days in an airtight container in the refrigerator.

To make a sandwich, cut a pita in half to form 2 pockets. Line each pocket with half a lettuce leaf. Spread 2 heaping tablespoons of feta spread into each pocket. Then fill each pocket with about 6 cucumber slices, 4 or 5 mint leaves, and 2 or 3 slices of chicken. Serve immediately or wrap in foil to go.

Makes 4 servings

Serving Size

2 pockets

Per Serving

Calories 370

Total Fat 9 g

Sat Fat 5 g Mono Fat 1.5 g Poly Fat 1 g

Protein 34 g

Carb 42 g

Fiber 6 g

Cholesterol 80 mg

Sodium 700 mg

Excellent Source of Calcium, Fiber, Iron, Magnesium, Manganese, Niacin, Phosphorus, Protein, Riboflavin, Selenium, Thiamin, Vitamin B6, Zinc.

THAILAND CHICKEN

Bring this sandwich for lunch and you'll be thinking about it all morning. You'll yearn for the sweet-spicy-creamy-sesame sauce and you'll anticipate the perfect balance between the crunch of the vegetables and the savory tenderness of the chicken.

For The Sauce :

- 3 tablespoons plain Greek-style nonfat yogurt
- 2 tablespoons mayonnaise
- tablespoon brown sugar
- 1 tablespoon low-sodium soy sauce
- 1 teaspoon Dijon mustard
- ½ teaspoon toasted sesame oil
- ¼ teaspoon Thai-style chili sauce (such as Sriracha) , optional

For The Sandwich

- 12 napa cabbage leaves, white center ribs removed
- 4 whole-wheat wrap breads (about 9 inches in diameter)
- 4 cooked chicken breast halves (about 5 ounces each) , sliced into ½ -inch-thick slices
- 1 red bell pepper, sliced into thin strips

To make the sauce, combine the yogurt, mayonnaise, brown sugar, soy sauce, mustard, sesame oil, and chili sauce, if using, and stir until well blended. The sauce will keep up to 5 days in an airtight container in the refrigerator.

To make each wrap, place 2 cabbage leaves on 1 wrap bread, then layer with a quarter of the chicken and peppers. Drizzle with 2 tablespoons of the sauce. Top with an additional cabbage leaf. Fold the bread about an inch over each end of the filling, then roll up. Serve or wrap in foil to go.

Makes 4 servings

Serving Size

1 wrap

Per Serving

Calories 390

Total Fat 12 g

Sat Fat 2 g Mono Fat 2.5 g Poly Fat 4 g

Protein 37

Carb 31 g

Fiber 3 g

Cholesterol 80 mg

Sodium 420 mg

Excellent Source of Niacin, Phosphorus, Protein, Selenium, Vitamin A, Vitamin B6, Vitamin C.

Good Source of Fiber, Iron.

CRUNCHY CHICKEN

Meaty chunks of chicken, crisp juicy apple, and the rich crunch of walnuts folded into a thick, creamy dressing form an indulgent combination of flavors and textures that, when tucked into a wrap, is satisfaction you can hold in your hand.

- ¼ cup walnuts
- 1/3 cup plain Greek-style nonfat yogurt
- 1 tablespoon mayonnaise
- 2 teaspoons fresh lemon juice
- 1 teaspoon Dijon mustard
- 1 teaspoon minced fresh thyme
- 1 cup cubed cooked chicken breast (about 1/2 pound)
- 1 medium apple, unpeeled and diced (about ¾ cup) Salt and freshly ground black pepper to taste
- 4 large leaves romaine lettuce, rinsed and patted dry
- 4 whole-wheat wrap breads (about 9 inches in diameter)

Toast the walnuts in a dry skillet over medium-high heat, stirring frequently, until fragrant, 3 to 5 minutes.

In a medium bowl, stir the yogurt, mayonnaise, lemon juice, mustard, and thyme until smooth. Fold in the chicken, toasted walnuts, and apples. Season with salt and pepper.

To make each wrap, place 1 lettuce leaf on 1 wrap bread, then spoon about ¾ cup of the chicken mixture on top. Fold the bread about an inch over each end of the filling, then roll up. Serve or wrap in foil to go.

Makes 4 servings

Serving Size

1 wrap

Per Serving

Calories 300

Total Fat 11 g

Sat Fat 1 g Mono Fat 1. 5 g Poly Fat 5 g

Protein 20 g

Carb 30 g

Fiber 3 g

Cholesterol 35 mg

Sodium 240 mg

Excellent Source of Niacin, Protein.

Good Source of Fiber, Manganese, Phosphorus, Selenium, Vitamin B6.

MEDITERRANEAN SEA FRUITS

Oceans away from your typical mayonnaise-y tuna salad, this one is inspired by the way canned tuna is prepared in the Mediterranean. You'll commonly find it there tossed with olives, onion, and fresh parsley in a lemon and olive oil dressing. Bursting with flavor, it brings out the absolute best in the fish. Once you try tuna this way, you might never go back.

- 2 (6-ounce) cans chunk light tuna in water, drained well
- ¼ cup chopped fresh parsley
- ¼ cup chopped pitted Calamata olives
- ¼ cup finely diced red onion

- 2 tablespoons extra-virgin olive oil
- 1 tablespoon fresh lemon juice
- ½ teaspoon finely grated lemon zest
- Salt and freshly ground black pepper to taste
- 12 leaves romaine lettuce, thick ribs removed
- 4 whole-wheat wrap breads (about 9 inches in diameter)
- 1 large ripe tomato, sliced into half moons

In a medium bowl, combine the tuna, parsley, olives, onion, oil, lemon juice, and zest. Add salt and pepper to taste.

To make each sandwich, place 3 lettuce leaves on a wrap bread. Top with 1/3 cup of the tuna salad and a few tomato slices. Fold the bread about an inch over each end of the filling, then roll up. Serve or wrap in foil to go.

Makes 4 servings

Serving Size

1 wrap

Per Serving

Calories 340

Total Fat 11 g

Sat Fat 1 g Mono Fat 6 g Poly Fat 1 g

Protein 31 g

Carb 29 g

Fiber 4 g

Cholesterol 0 mg

Sodium 50 mg

Excellent Source of Protein, Vitamin A, Vitamin C, Vitamin D, Vitamin K.

Good Source of Fiber, Iron.

STEAK BEEF SANDWICH WITH HERBS AND TASTY SAUCE

Why settle for the same old roast beef sandwich when you can have one that's truly extraordinary with so little effort? What makes this one a standout are the zingy horseradish sauce that takes seconds to make, the peppery watercress that stands up so well to it, and pumpernickel bread that gives an unmistakable depth of flavor. Together they bring out the best in each other and the savory beef.

For The Sauce

- ¼ cup plain Greek-style nonfat yogurt
- ¼ cup prepared white horseradish, squeezed of excess juice (about 3 tablespoons)
- 2 tablespoons mayonnaise
- ¼ teaspoon salt
- 1/8 teaspoon freshly ground black pepper

For The Sandwich

- 1 bunch watercress, thick stems removed
- 8 slices pumpernickel bread
- ¾ pound lean roast beef, thinly sliced
- 2 medium tomatoes, sliced
- ½ small red onion, thinly sliced

To make the sauce, combine the yogurt, horseradish, mayonnaise, salt, and pepper in a small bowl and stir to incorporate. The sauce will keep for up to 5 days in an airtight container in the refrigerator.

To make each sandwich, place ¼ cup of watercress on a slice of bread and drizzle with 2 tablespoons of the sauce. Layer with a few slices of roast beef, then some of the tomato and onion slices. Top with another slice of bread and serve or wrap in foil to go.

Makes 4 servings

Serving Size

1 sandwich

Per Serving

Calories 360

Total Fat 9 g

Sat Fat 2 g Mono Fat 0.5 g Poly Fat 1 g

Protein 25 g

Carb 39 g

Fiber 5 g

Cholesterol 30 mg

Sodium 1290 mg

Excellent Source of Fiber, Manganese, Protein, Selenium, Vitamin C, Vitamin K.

Good Source of Calcium, Copper, Folate, Iron, Magnesium, Niacin, Phosphorus, Riboflavin, Thiamin, Vitamin A .

TUNA STUFFED WITH FRESH HERBS

Sweet, crisp red peppers make the perfect edible serving cups for lemony tuna salad piled with fresh herbs. It will bring an energizing burst of garden freshness to you wherever you choose to eat it.

- 4 red bell peppers, stemmed and sliced in half crosswise
- ¼ cup extra-virgin olive oil
- 3 tablespoons fresh lemon juice
- 2 teaspoons Dijon mustard
- ½ teaspoon salt
- ¼ teaspoon freshly ground black pepper
- 4 (6-ounce) cans chunk light tuna in water, drained
- 1 ½ cups lightly packed baby arugula leaves, roughly chopped
- 1 cup lightly packed fresh basil leaves, minced
- 1 cup lightly packed fresh parsley leaves, minced
- 3 tablespoons loosely packed fresh tarragon, minced

Using a paring knife, remove the seeds and white membrane from inside the pepper halves.

In a large bowl, combine the olive oil, lemonjuice, mustard, salt, and pepper and whisk to incorporate. Add the tuna, arugula, and minced herbs and stir to incorporate. Spoon about V2 cup of the tuna mixture into each pepper half and serve, or place 2 filled peppers in each to-go container. Filled peppers will keep up to 2 days in an airtight container in the refrigerator.

Makes 4 servings

Serving Size

2 filled pepper halves

Per Serving

Calories 380

Total Fat 15 g

Sat Fat 2 g Mono Fat 10 g Poly Fat 2 g

Protein 47 g

Carb 9 g

Fiber 3 g

Cholesterol 105 mg

Sodium 1020 mg

Excellent Source of Protein, Vitamin A, Vitamin C, Vitamin K.

Good Source of Fiber, Folate, Manganese, Potassium, Vitamin B6.

Canned tuna is a delicious, convenient lean protein that is rich in omega-3 fats. Trouble is, some varieties can have high levels of mercury, a toxic environmental pollutant. Stick with light tuna, which has about a third the mercury of albacore or chunk white, and you can safely have up to three cans a week.

SHRIMP SOUP-CREAM

This refreshing, zesty, cold tomato soup couldn't be simpler to make. All you do is take garden fresh ingredients, whir them in the blender, and voila! Plump bites of shrimp and some crusty bread make it a satisfying meal. It is as good in a packed lunch as it is served in large cocktail glasses as an elegant appetizer.

- 2 scallions
- 1 English cucumber (about 1 pound), seeded and cut into chunks
- 1 large red or orange bell pepper, cored, seeded and cut into chunks
- ¼ teaspoon finely chopped garlic
- 1 quart low-sodium tomato juice
- 4 medium tomatoes (about 1 pound), diced
- 2 tablespoons extra-virgin olive oil
- 4 teaspoons red wine vinegar, or more to taste
- Salt and freshly ground black pepper to taste
- Hot sauce, to taste
- ½ pound cooked peeled shrimp, cut into ½ -inch pieces
- Crusty whole-wheat bread

Thinly slice the green portion of 1 scallion and reserve for garnish. Cut the remaining white portion and whole scallion into chunks. In the bowl of a food processor, combine the scallion, cucumber, bell pepper, and garlic. Pulse until the vegetables are coarsely chopped.

Add the tomato juice and pulse until the vegetables are finely chopped. Transfer to a large bowl and stir in the diced tomatoes, olive oil, and vinegar. Season to taste with salt, pepper, and hot sauce.

Gazpacho will keep for up to 5 days in an airtight container in the refrigerator.

To serve, transfer the soup to individual bowls or to-go containers. Right before eating, top with the chopped shrimp and scallion greens. Serve with the bread.

Makes 4 servings

Serving Size

2 cups plus 2 slices bread

Per Serving

Calories 370

Total Fat 10 g

Sat Fat 1 g Mono Fat 5 g Poly Fat 1.5 g

Protein 23 g

Carb 48 g

Fiber 11 g

Cholesterol 11 0 mg

Sodium 630 mg

Excellent Source of Copper, Fiber, Folate, Iron, Niacin, Potassium, Protein, Selenium, Thiamin, Vitamin A, Vitamin B6, Vitamin C, Vitamin D, Vitamin K.

Good Source of Magnesium, Manganese, Phosphorus, Riboflavin, Vitamin B12, Zinc.

RAVIOLI-SPINACH SOUP

Who says a meal on the go has to be cold? Get yourself a good wide- mouthed thermos and you can have a belly-warming lunch anytime. This simple recipe is soup-er satisfying thanks to the plump cheese- filled pasta.

- 1 teaspoon canola oil
- 1 medium onion, chopped (about 2 cups)
- 2 cloves garlic, thinly sliced
- large carrot, peeled and sliced (1 ½ cups)

- ribs celery, chopped (1 cup)
- 1 teaspoon dried oregano
- 1 teaspoon dried thyme
- ½ teaspoon crushed red pepper flakes
- 1 (14-ounce) can low-sodium diced tomatoes, with juice
- 6 cups low-sodium chicken broth or vegetable broth
- ounces baby spinach, sliced into ribbons (3 cups)
- 1 (9-ounce) package fresh store-bought spinach-and-cheese ravioli (2 cups)
- ½ cup grated Parmesan cheese (1 ½ ounces)

Heat the oil in a 4- or 6-quart saucepan over medium-high heat. Add the onions and cook, stirring, until softened, about 5 minutes. Add the garlic and cook, stirring, until the onions are translucent and the garlic is softened, another 3 minutes. Add the carrot, celery, oregano, thyme, and red pepper flakes and cook, stirring, until softened, 5 to 6 minutes.

Add the tomatoes with their juices and the broth and bring to a boil; reduce the heat and simmer for 10 to 15 minutes. Add the spinach and ravioli and cook until the ravioli are cooked through, 6 minutes. This soup will keep for up to 3 days in the refrigerator in an airtight container. Serve topped with Parmesan cheese.

For a lunch to go, put the warm soup into a wide-mouth thermal container designed to hold food. Pack the Parmesan cheese in a separate small bag. And don't forget a spoon!

Makes 4 servings

Serving Size

3 cups soup plus 2 tablespoons Parmesan cheese

Per Serving

Calories 390

Total Fat 12 g

Sat Fat 5 g Mono Fat 1. 75 g Poly Fat 1 g

Protein 25 g

Carb 45 g

Fiber 6 g

Cholesterol 45 mg

Sodium 760 mg

Excellent Source of Calcium, Fiber, Iron, Niacin, Protein, Vitamin A, Vitamin C, Vitamin K

Good Source of Copper, Phosphorus, Potassium

.

LUNCH AT HOME

Melted cheese is the first thing that comes to mind when I am home for lunch. It is one of those luxurious, fresh-out-of-the-oven elements you just have to be home to do. And this chapter has its tantalizing share-from quick grilled sandwiches to easy pizzas and frittatas. But lunch at home also means foods that are best enjoyed just cut, like avocado, or just cooked, like crunchy potato chips. And it means you might have company you want to wow with a beautiful presentation, without having to work too hard, of course. Whether it's a day off and you have a little extra time or you just have a quick break between errands or home office work, there is a perfect lunch here to eat right at home.

PROSCIUTOO & CHEESE SANDWICH

Grilled ham and cheese is an everyday, easy lunch fallback taken to a new level here with tender prosciutto, intensely flavorful provolone cheese, and peppery radicchio toasted to melty perfection on crusty bread.

- 1 (8-ounce) loaf whole-grain Italian bread
- 2 tablespoons balsamic vinegar
- 12 radicchio leaves 16 large basil leaves
- 4 ounces thinly sliced prosciutto
- 4 slices provolone cheese (4 ounces)
- ¼ teaspoon freshly ground black pepper
- 2 teaspoons olive oil
- Cooking spray

Slice the bread loaf in half lengthwise. Scoop out the bread to remove the soft inner portion and discard. Slice the loaf crosswise into 4 equal-size pieces. Drizzle the inside of each roll with 1 ½ teaspoons of the vinegar. Layer 3 radicchio leaves, 4 basil leaves, 1 ounce of prosciutto, and 1 ounce of provolone in each roll. Sprinkle with the pepper. Close the rolls and brush each panini with ½ teaspoon of the olive oil.

Heat a heavy cast-iron skillet or other skillet over medium-high heat and spray with cooking spray. Place 2 sandwiches in the skillet and weigh them down with another skillet or a panini weight. Toast until the cheese begins to melt and the bread is browned and toasted on the edges, 3 to 4 minutes. Flip the sandwiches and toast for an additional 2 to 3 minutes. Remove from the pan and slice in half; repeat with the remaining 2 sandwiches.

Makes 4 servings

Serving Size

1 sandwich

Per Serving

Calories 290

Total Fat 15 g

Sat Fat 6 g Mono Fat 4 g Poly Fat 0.5 g

Protein 23 g

Carb 22 g

Fiber 4 g

Cholesterol 40 mg

Sodium 1200 mg

Excellent Source of Calcium, Protein, Vitamin K Good Source of Fiber, Folate, Niacin, Phosphorus, Riboflavin, Thiamin.

Eating Well Tip

Scooping out the inside of your crusty bread leaves you more room for the goodies inside your sandwich, and has 25 percent fewer calories than unscooped bread.

GREEK PIZZA WITH LAMB AND SALAD

Just about every group of people around the world eats some kind of pizza. This version hails from the Middle East, with rich ground lamb fragrant with cinnamon, topped with crunchy pine nuts and salty feta cheese, and baked atop crisp pita bread, the ultimate no-fuss crust.

- 1 small onion, chopped (about 1 cup)
- 8 ounces lean ground lamb
- 4 medium plum tomatoes, chopped
- 2 tablespoons chopped fresh parsley
- ¾ teaspoon ground cinnamon
- ¾ teaspoon salt
- ½ teaspoon freshly ground black pepper
- 4 whole-wheat pita breads
- 2 teaspoons olive oil
- 1/3 cup crumbled feta cheese
- 1 tablespoon pine nuts

Preheat the oven to 400°F.

Put the onion and ground lamb into a large skillet over medium-high heat and cook, breaking the meat up with a spoon and stirring occasionally, until the onion is softened and the meat is no longer pink, about 5 minutes. Transfer the meat and onion to a plate lined with paper towels to drain the fat. Blot with an additional paper towel.

Wipe out the pan and return the meat and onion to the pan. Stir in the tomatoes, and cook over medium-high heat until the tomatoes soften slightly, about 2 minutes. Remove from the heat. Stir in the parsley, cinnamon, salt, and pepper. The lamb mixture may be made up to 2 days ahead and stored in an airtight container in the refrigerator.

Place the pita breads on a baking sheet. Brush the top of each pita with oil. Spread 1/3 cup of the lamb mixture onto each pita. Sprinkle with the feta and pine nuts. Cook until the cheese is warmed and softened and the pita is toasted, 10 to 12 minutes. Serve alongside the Fennel- Arugula Salad.

Makes 4 servings

Serving Size

1 pita pizza and 1½ cups salad

Per Serving

Calories 500

Total Fat 29 g

Sat Fat 9 g Mono Fat 13 g Poly Fat 4 g

Protein 22 g

Carb 48 g

Fiber 8 g

Cholesterol 55 mg

Sodium 11 40 mg

Excellent Source of Fiber, Folate, Iron, Magnesium, Manganese, Niacin, Phosphorus, Potassium, Protein, Riboflavin, Selenium, Thiamin, Vitamin A, Vitamin B6, Vitamin B12, Vitamin C, Vitamin K, Zinc.

Good Source of Copper, Pantothenic Acid.

FENNEL-ARUGULA SALAD

This refreshing salad is the perfect complement to the deep flavors of the lamb pizza.

- 1 medium bulb fennel, thinly sliced into half-moons
- 6 cups arugula (6 ounces)
- 2 tablespoons extra-virgin olive oil
- 3 tablespoons orange juice
- 1 tablespoons red wine vinegar
- 1 tablespoon finely chopped shallot
- ½ teaspoon finely grated orange zest
- ¼ teaspoon salt
- ¼ teaspoon freshly ground black pepper

Toss the fennel and arugula together in a large salad bowl. In a small bowl, whisk together the oil, orange juice, vinegar, shallot, orange zest, salt, and pepper. Add to the fennel and arugula and toss to coat.

Makes 4 servings

Serving Size

1 ½ cups

PIZZA ALL-IN

I was in Italy the first time I had egg on a pizza. The idea seemed odd, but when I tried it, it was a revelation. When you cut into the egg, the yolk oozes out over the tender greens and crisp crust. With prosciutto and Parmesan packing a serious flavor punch, this is real Italian pizza like you never knew before. Store-bought crust and pre-washed spinach make this recipe practically effortless.

- 1 store-bought baked thin-crust pizza crust (preferably whole-wheat; such as Boboli)
- 4 cups baby spinach leaves, thinly sliced, (about 4 ounces)
- 2 teaspoons olive oil
- 3 ounces thinly sliced prosciutto, cut into thin strips
- ½ cup grated Parmesan cheese (1 ½ ounces)
- 3 cloves garlic, thinly sliced
- 4 large eggs

Preheat the oven to 450°F.

Place the pizza crust on a baking sheet. Scatter the spinach all over the crust and drizzle with the oil. Evenly distribute the prosciutto, Parmesan, and garlic on top of the spinach. Make 4 wells in the spinach topping, spacing them so there is 1 well on each quarter of the pizza. Crack 1 egg into each of the wells.

Bake for 12 to 15 minutes, until the spinach is wilted and the egg whites are fully cooked. Cut into 4 large slices.

Makes 4 servings

Serving Size

1 slice

Per Serving

Calories 400

Total Fat 17 g

Sat Fat 5 g

Mono Fat 1.5 g Poly Fat 0.5 g

Protein 29 g

Carb 38 g

Fiber 6 g

Cholesterol 240 mg

Sodium 1280 mg

Excellent Source of Calcium, Fiber, Protein, Vitamin A, Vitamin K.

Good Source of Folate, Iron, Manganese, Vitamin C.

SPAGHETTI OMLETTE WITH SALAD PRESTO

A frittata is basically a crustless quiche-all the custard-y vegetable- studded egg filling without the fuss or fat of a pastry. In this recipe, marinara-laced spaghetti adds an extra layer of flavor and satisfaction. What a great way to use leftover pasta and sauce !

- 5 large eggs
- 5 large egg whites
- 1 tablespoon olive oil
- 1 small onion, sliced thinly into half moons
- 5 cups baby spinach leaves
- ¼ cup sun-dried tomatoes (not oil-packed) , reconstituted in boiling water for 10 minutes, chopped
- 1 large clove garlic, minced
- ½ teaspoon salt
- ¼ teaspoon freshly ground black pepper
- 2 cups cooked whole-wheat spaghetti (4 ounces dry spaghetti) , tossed with ½ cup marinara sauce
- 1/3 cup grated Parmesan cheese
- 1 recipe Salad Presto

In a medium bowl, whisk together the eggs and egg whites.

Heat the oil in a large ovenproof, nonstick skillet over medium-high heat. Add the onion and cook, stirring occasionally, until softened, 3 to 5 minutes. Add the spinach, sun-dried tomatoes, garlic, salt, and pepper and cook, stirring, until the spinach is wilted, about 1 minute. Add the spaghetti to the pan and stir to combine. Pour the eggs evenly over the spaghetti and vegetables. Lower the heat to medium-low and cook until the eggs are set on the edges but not in the middle, 6 to 8 minutes.

Preheat the broiler. Sprinkle the top of the frittata with cheese and place under the broiler. Cook until the top is set and golden brown, 2 to 3 minutes; be careful not to overcook or the eggs will become tough. Cut into 8 wedges and serve with the Salad Presto.

Makes 4 servings

Serving Size

2 wedges and 1 cup salad

Per Serving

Calories 400

Total Fat 20 g

Sat Fat 5 g Mono Fat 8 g Poly Fat 2 g

Protein 23 g

Carb 34 g

Fiber 7 g

Cholesterol 275 mg

Sodium 810 mg

Excellent Source of Calcium, Fiber, Iron, Manganese, Protein, Selenium, Vitamin A, Vitamin C.

Good Source of Iodine, Riboflavin.

SALAD PRESTO

Just open a bag of greens, whisk up some oil and vinegar, and there you have it. Salad, presto ! You don't even need to take out a knife. Its crisp bright flavor goes perfectly with the frittata.

- 1 (5-ounce) bag mixed greens (5 cups lightly packed)
- 3 tablespoons extra-virgin olive oil
- 1 tablespoon red wine vinegar
- Pinch of dried basil
- Salt and freshly ground black pepper to taste

Put the greens in a medium salad bowl. In a separate bowl, whisk together the oil and vinegar. Drizzle the dressing over the greens and sprinkle the dried basil on top. Season with salt and pepper. Serve.

Makes 4 servings

Serving Size

1 cup

CHICKEN PAILLARD WITH HERBS & TOMATO SALAD

Thin-cut chicken breast is a great shortcut here. It eliminates the need to pound the chicken out and it cooks up in minutes. Topped with a beautiful lemony watercress salad, this dish has real flair, and you barely have to lift a finger.

- 1 ¼ pounds thin-cut skinless boneless chicken breasts
- 3 tablespoons extra-virgin olive oil
- 1 clove garlic, minced
- ¾ teaspoon salt
- ¾ teaspoon freshly ground black pepper
- 3 tablespoons fresh lemon juice
- 1 large bunch watercress, tough stems removed, coarsely chopped (about 4 cups)
- 2 medium tomatoes, chopped
- 8 slices whole-grain baguette

Combine the chicken, 1 tablespoon of the olive oil, the garlic, and ½ teaspoon each of the salt and pepper in a bowl and toss to coat.

Preheat a grill or nonstick grill pan over medium-high heat. Grill the chicken until grill marks form and the meat is just cooked through, 2 to 3 minutes per side. Remove from the grill and sprinkle with 1 tablespoon of the lemon juice.

In a large bowl, toss the watercress and tomatoes, with their seeds, with the remaining 2 tablespoons of each olive oil and lemon juice, and the remaining ¼ teaspoon of each salt and pepper. Distribute the chicken among 4 serving plates and top each with 1 ½ cups of the salad and 1 to 2 tablespoons of accumulated liquid from the salad.

Serve with the baguette slices.

Makes 4 servings

Serving Size

4 ounces cooked chicken breast, 1 ½ cups salad, and 2 pieces bread

Per Serving

Calories 270

Total Fat 14 g

Sat Fat 2.5 g Mono Fat 8.5 g Poly Fat 2 g

Protein 32 g

Carb 4 g

Fiber 1 g

Cholesterol 80 mg

Sodium 520 mg

Excellent Source of Niacin, Phosphorus, Protein, Selenium, Vitamin A, Vitamin B6, Vitamin C, Vitamin K.

Good Source of Magnesium, Pantothenic Acid, Potassium.

GRILLED BEEF WITH APPLE SALAD

This Thai-inspired salad has that classic tart-sweet-spicy flavor balance that really gets your taste buds dancing. The cool, crunchy herb-laced salad is the yin to the yang of the rich tender beef. What's more, the food processor does most of the work.

- 1 ¼ pounds shoulder center steak (ranch steak) or top sirloin steak, boneless
- 1 teaspoon salt
- ¼ teaspoon freshly ground black pepper
- ¼ cup fresh lime juice
- ¼ cup rice vinegar
- 2 tablespoons sugar
- 1 large jicama (about 1 ½ pounds), peeled
- 2 green apples (about 1 pound), cored
- ½ cup fresh cilantro leaves, plus more for garnish
- 2 teaspoons finely grated lime zest
- 1 medium jalapeno pepper, seeded and diced (about 2 teaspoons)
- 3 tablespoons chopped roasted peanuts

Heat a grill pan over medium-high heat. Season the steak with the salt and pepper and grill until medium-rare, 3 to 4 minutes per side. Let the meat rest for 5 minutes, then cut across the grain into ¼-inch-thick slices.

In a small bowl, combine the lime juice, vinegar, and sugar and whisk until the sugar is partially dissolved. Using the shredder attachment of a food processor, shred the jicama and apples; transfer to a bowl. Add the cilantro, lime zest, jalapeno, and dressing, and toss to combine.

To serve, mound 1 ½ ups of the salad into each serving bowl and top with about 7 slices of beef. Garnish each bowl with additional cilantro leaves and about 2 teaspoons of toasted peanuts. Serve immediately.

Makes 4 servings

Serving Size

1 ½ cups salad, about 7 slices beef, and 2 teaspoons peanuts

Per Serving

Calories 370

Total Fat 11 g

Sat Fat 3.5 g Mono Fat 4.5 g Poly Fat 1.5 g

Protein 34 g

Carb 37 g

Fiber 11 g

Cholesterol 50 mg

Sodium 670 mg

Excellent Source of Fiber, Iron, Niacin, Phosphorus, Potassium, Protein, Selenium, Vitamin B6, Vitamin B12, Vitamin C, Zinc.

Good Source of Copper, Folate, Magnesium, Manganese, Pantothenic Acid, Riboflavin, Thiamin, Vitamin K.

STRAWBERRY AND CHEESE SALAD

I get a kick out of using everyday ingredients in unexpected ways. The result is something exciting and different but not too far out of the comfort zone. This dish is a fresh take on the traditional Italian tomato and mozzarella salad. The juicy berries are a fragrant complement to the creamy, soft cheese, and the balsamic vinegar adds just the right touch of sweetness.

- ¼ cup extra-virgin olive oil
- 2 tablespoons balsamic vinegar
- ¼ teaspoon salt

- ¼ teaspoon freshly ground pepper
- 2 hearts of romaine lettuce, torn or cut into bite-size pieces (5 lightly packed cups)
- 1 (1 6-ounce) container fresh strawberries, hulled and sliced
- 6 ounces part-skim mozzarella cheese, diced (about 1 ½ cups)
- ½ cup lightly packed fresh basil leaves, cut into ribbons
- 8 slices whole-grain Italian bread

In a small bowl, whisk together the oil, vinegar, salt, and pepper. Place the lettuce in a large bowl and toss with half of the dressing.

Place the lettuce on 4 salad plates. Toss the strawberries with the remaining dressing and place ¼ of the berries on top of each mound of lettuce. Top each with cheese, then sprinkle with the basil. Serve the bread alongside.

Makes 4 servings

Serving Size

3 cups salad and 2 pieces bread

Per Serving

Calories 400

Total Fat 25 g

Sat Fat 8 g Mono Fat 10 g

Poly Fat 3 g Protein 16 g

Carb 36 g

Fiber 4 g

Cholesterol 30 mg

Sodium 720 mg

Excellent Source of Calcium, Folate, Manganese, Protein, Vitamin A, Vitamin C, Vitamin K

Good Source of Fiber, Iron, Niacin, Selenium, Thiamin

CLUB SALAD

This salad definitely has the wow factor with colorful rows of scrumptious goodies adorning a bed of crisp lettuce. It seems too decadent to be healthful, but a few simple tricks, like crisping the smoked ham in a skillet to give a bacon-like effect, make it as good for you as it tastes.

For The Dressing

- 3 tablespoons extra-virgin olive oil
- 2 tablespoons red wine vinegar
- 1 tablespoon fresh lemon juice
- 1 teaspoon Dijon mustard
- 1 teaspoon Worcestershire sauce
- 1 small clove garlic, minced
- ¼ teaspoon salt
- ¼ teaspoon freshly ground black pepper

For The Salad

- ¼ pound sliced Black Forest ham
- cooking spray
- hard-boiled eggs
- 6 cups coarsely chopped romaine lettuce (about 6 ounces)
- 2 cups watercress, thick stems removed
- 2 medium tomatoes, seeded and diced (about 2 cups)
- ½ avocado, pitted, peeled and diced (about ¾ cup)
- 1 cup cooked diced chicken breast
- ½ cup crumbled Roquefort or blue cheese (about 2 ounces)

In a small bowl, whisk together all of the dressing ingredients.

Slice the ham into ½ -inch strips. Spray a nonstick skillet with cooking spray and preheat it over medium-high heat. Cook the ham in the skillet, stirring frequently, until crisped, 3 to 5 minutes. Remove from the heat.

Remove and discard the yolk from one of the hard-boiled eggs. Chop the remaining egg white and whole egg and set aside.

In a large bowl, toss the romaine and watercress with two-thirds of the dressing. Put the dressed greens on a large serving dish. Place the tomatoes, avocado, chicken, cheese, diced egg, and the crisped ham on top of the greens. Drizzle with the remaining dressing.

Makes 4 servings

Serving Size

3 cups

Per Serving

Calories 370

Total Fat 24 g

Sat Fat 7 g Mono Fat 13 g Poly Fat 3 g

Protein 26 g

Carb 11 g

Fiber 4 g

Cholesterol 11 0 mg

Sodium 760 mg

Excellent Source of Folate, Niacin, Phosphorus, Protein, Riboflavin, Selenium, Thiamin, Vitamin A, Vitamin B6, Vitamin C, Vitamin K.

Good Source of Calcium, Fiber, Iodine, Iron, Magnesium, Manganese, Pantothenic Acid, Potassium, Vitamin B12, Zinc.

CRAB AND AVOCADO COMBO WITH COOL CUCUMBER SOUP

This stack of rich, succulent crab and creamy avocado is impressive and rich tasting yet barely counts as cooking. It is reallyjust pulling together the best of nature and presenting it in an artful, inspired way. The funny thing is, you achieve such elegance with a very unfancy tool-an empty can. I like to serve this as part of a light summer luncheon after the Cool Cucumber Soup.

- 1 ripe avocado
- 3 tablespoons fresh lemon juice
- ¼ teaspoon salt, plus more to taste
- 1 teaspoon Dijon mustard
- Pinch of ground white pepper
- ½ pound lump crabmeat
- 2 tablespoons chopped chives
- 8 slices whole-grain baguette

Pit and peel the avocado and cut it into ½ -inch chunks. In a small bowl, toss the avocado chunks gently with I tablespoon of the lemon juice and season with salt to taste. In a medium bowl, whisk together the remaining 2 tablespoons of lemon juice, the Dijon mustard, white pepper, and the ¼ teaspoon of salt. Add the crabmeat and toss.

For a decorative presentation, stand an empty (15-ounce) can (with both the top and bottom removed) on a serving plate. Scoop a quarter of the avocado into the can, being careful to avoid any sharp edge on the rim. Place a quarter of the crabmeat on top and press down gently into the can. Gently pull the can off the avocado and crab mixture.

Garnish with ½ tablespoon of the chives. Repeat with the remaining three servings and serve with the bread alongside or following the Cool Cucumber Soup.

Makes 4 servings

Serving Size

1 "combo," 1 cup soup, and 2 slices of bread

Per Serving

Calories 380

Total Fat 12 g

Sat Fat 2 g Mono Fat 7 g Poly Fat 2 g

Protein 29 g

Carb 43 g

Fiber 7 g

Cholesterol 70 mg

Sodium 760 mg

Excellent Source of Calcium, Fiber, Folate, Potassium, Protein, Vitamin C, Vitamin K.

Good Source of Copper, Iron, Magnesium, Manganese, Niacin, Pantothenic Acid, Phosphorus, Riboflavin, Selenium, Thiamin, Vitamin A, Vitamin B6.

FRESH CUCUMBER SOUP

If you could sip a refreshing summer breeze, this is what it would taste like. You'll stay cool making it because all you have to do is put the ingredients in a blender and whir.

- 3 cups plain nonfat yogurt
- 1 English cucumber (about 1 pound), cut into chunks
- 1 scallion (white and green parts), coarsely chopped (about ¼ cup)
- 3 tablespoons chopped fresh dill, plus more for garnish
- Salt and freshly ground black pepper to taste
- 1 medium tomato (about 5 ounces), seeded and diced
- 2 teaspoons extra-virgin olive oil

In a blender, combine the yogurt, cucumber, scallion, and dill. Pulse until pureed. Season to taste with salt and pepper. Ladle into individual bowls. Top each serving with 2 tablespoons of diced tomato, drizzle with V2 teaspoon of olive oil, and garnish with a dill sprig.

Makes 4 servings

Serving Size

1 cup soup with 2 slices bread

SHRIMP ROLL WITH CRACKED SPICY POTATO CHIPS

This classic shrimp salad heaped onto a toasted hot dog bun served alongside warm, homemade potato chips is fun food that tastes seriously good.

- 1/3 cup plain Greek-style nonfat yogurt
- 3 tablespoons mayonnaise
- 1 stalk celery, finely chopped
- tablespoon chopped scallion greens (from about 1 scallion)
- 1 tablespoon fresh lemon juice
- 1 pound cooked shelled medium shrimp
- Salt and freshly ground black pepper to taste
- chilli powder to taste
- 4 whole-wheat hot dog buns
- 1 tablespoon extra-virgin olive oil

In a bowl, stir together the yogurt, mayonnaise, celery, scallions, and lemon juice. Fold in the shrimp and season to taste with salt, pepper and chilli powder. Chill until ready to use. Just before serving, open the hot dog buns and brush the inside with olive oil. Heat a grill pan over medium- high heat and grill the bread, cut side down, until toasted, about 3 minutes. Fill each with ¾ cup of the shrimp mixture and serve immediately with Cracked Pepper Potato Chips.

Makes 4 servings

Serving Size

1 shrimp roll and about 15 potato chips

Per Serving

Calories 530

Total Fat 19 g

Sat Fat 3 g Mono Fat 8.5 g Poly Fat 7 g

Protein 34 g

Carb 57 g

Fiber 7 g

Cholesterol 225 mg

Sodium 560 mg

Excellent Source of Copper, Fiber, Iron, Magnesium, Manganese, Niacin, Phosphorus, Potassium, Protein, Selenium, Vitamin B6, Vitamin B12, Vitamin C, Vitamin D, Zinc.

Good Source of Calcium, Folate, Pantothenic Acid, Riboflavin, Thiamin, Vitamin K.

Tip

Keep frozen cleaned shrimp on hand, both cooked and uncooked, for a quick, easy, and upscale protein, there when you need it.

CRACKED AND SPICY PEPPER POTATO CHIPS

Imagine, chips that are good for you! Just a touch of oil and some oven time make these potato rounds crispy and even more addictive than the packaged kind. A devilish sprinkle of pepper deters my daughter so there are more for me.

- 2 large russet potatoes (1 ¾ pounds total) , sliced into 1/8-inch-thick rounds
- 1 tablespoon plus 1 teaspoon olive oil
- 1 teaspoon coarsely ground black pepper
- 1 teaspon chill powder

Salt to taste

Preheat the oven to 450°F. Toss the potatoes in a large bowl with the oil, pepper and chilli powder until well coated. Arrange the potato slices in 1 layer on a baking sheet; use 2 baking sheets if necessary. Bake for 20 to 25 minutes, until chips are crisped and lightly browned. Remove from the oven, season with salt, and cool.

Makes 4 servings

Serving Size

About 15 chips

CHICKEN CHEESY SANDWICH

What sounds more appealing than a chicken Parm sandwich, drowning in melted cheese and zesty marinara sauce atop toasted Italian bread? How about knowing that with the right ingredients on hand you can have it on the table in less than 10 minutes, and it's good for you, too!

- 1 loaf whole-grain Italian bread (about 8 ounces)
- 2 cups jarred marinara sauce
- 4 (5-ounce) cooked skinless boneless chicken breasts
- 4 cups baby spinach leaves
- 1 cup shredded part-skim mozzarella cheese (4 ounces)

- ¼ cup grated Parmesan cheese (3/4 ounce)

Preheat the broiler.

Slice the bread in half lengthwise, then in half again crosswise so you wind up with 4 pieces. Scoop out the bread to remove the soft inner portion and discard. Place the bread scooped side up on a baking tray. Spoon V! cup of sauce into each piece of bread. Lay a piece of chicken on top and cover with 1 cup of spinach leaves. Pour another V! cup of sauce on top of the spinach, then sprinkle each sandwich with V! cup of mozzarella and 1 tablespoon of Parmesan.

Broil until the spinach is wilted and the cheese is bubbly and browned, 4 to 5 minutes.

Makes 4 servings

Serving Size

piece

Per Serving

Calories 430

Total Fat 12 g

Sat Fat 5 g Mono Fat 3 g

Poly Fat 1. 5 g Protein 44 g

Carb 35 g

Fiber 5 g

Cholesterol 100 mg

Sodium 1090 mg

Excellent Source of Calcium, Folate, Iron, Niacin, Phosphorus, Protein, Selenium, Vitamin A, Vitamin B6, Vitamin C.

Good Source of Fiber, Magnesium, Manganese, Pantothenic Acid, Riboflavin, Thiamin, Vitamin B12, Zinc.

Tip:

Sure, it is easy to make a basic tomato sauce from scratch, but sometimes you need a shortcut, and jarred sauce can be your ticket to a fantastic meal in no time. The trick is to buy a good one. Here are some things to look for:

- olive oil instead of other oils
- no preservatives, stabilizers, or artificial ingredients
- less than 500 mg of sodium, 6 grams of sugar, and 4 grams of fat per V2 cup

RUSH HOUR DINNER

If most days are so busy you are lucky to get a home-heated meal on the table, much less a home-cooked one, here comes the cavalry: 25 complete dinners you can whip up in about 30 minutes or less.

Each is inspired, absolutely delicious, family friendly, and good for you-All in less time than it takes to order a pizza. They are the kind of dinners that magnetically draw people together around the table and leave everyone marveling about how you manage to do it all so well. It's maximum reward for minimum effort.

MULTI-COLOR PEPPER STEAK

Sweet, savory sauteed onions and peppers with strips of steak in a mouthwatering sauce, all ready in 20 minutes using just one pan. This is destined to become one of your go-to dinners.

- 4 teaspoons canola oil
- 1 ¼ pounds top round, London broil, or flank steak, thinly sliced
- 5 large assorted bell peppers (such as a mixture of red, yellow, and green; about 2 pounds total)
- 1 large onion, sliced into half moons (about 3 cups) 4 cloves garlic, sliced
- 1 ½ cups low-sodium beef broth
- 1 ½ cup dry red wine
- 3 tablespoons low-sodium soy sauce
- ½ teaspoon freshly ground black pepper
- 1 ½ teaspoons cornstarch, dissolved in ¼ cup cold water 3 cups cooked brown rice

Heat 2 teaspoons of the oil in a large skillet over medium-high heat. Add the beef and cook until browned on all sides, about 5 minutes. Transfer the meat with its juices to a plate.

Heat the remaining 2 teaspoons of oil in the same skillet over medium-high heat. Add the peppers and onion and cook, stirring occasionally, for 5 minutes. Add the garlic and continue cooking until the peppers are softened and onions are translucent, about 5 minutes more.

Return the beef and juices to the skillet and add the broth, wine, soy sauce, and pepper. Bring to a boil. Reduce the heat and simmer until the liquid has reduced by half, about 5 minutes. Stir in the dissolved cornstarch and cook until the mixture thickens, about 2 minutes. Serve over the rice.

Makes 4 servings

Serving Size

2 cups pepper steak plus ¼ cup sauce, ¾ cup brown rice

Per Serving

Calories 540

Total Fat 14 g

Sat Fat 4 g Mono Fat 6.5 g Poly Fat 2 g

Protein 40 g

Carb 56 g

Fiber 7 g

Cholesterol 50 mg

Sodium 410 mg

Excellent Source of Copper, Fiber, Folate, Iron, Magnesium, Manganese, Niacin, Pantothenic Acid, Phosphorus, Potassium, Protein, Riboflavin, Selenium, Thiamin, Vitamin A, Vitamin B6, Vitamin B12, Vitamin C, Zinc.

Good Source of Vitamin K.

RUSSIAN BEEF WITH FRESH GREEN BEANS AND GRAINY MUSTARD

This dish is old-fashioned goodness for the modern-day dinner rush. Tender beef with mushrooms in creamy sauce over noodles-it's just like grandma's only better for you and a cinch to make.

- 4 teaspoons canola oil
- 1 pound top round, London broil, or flank steak, thinly sliced
- 1 small onion, thinly sliced
- 2 (8-ounce) packages white button mushrooms, cleaned, stemmed, and sliced (about 5 cups)
- 2 cloves garlic, minced
- 1 tablespoon all-purpose flour
- 2 cups low-sodium beef broth
- ½ cup dry red wine
- ¾ teaspoon salt
- ½ teaspoon freshly ground black pepper
- 2/3 cup plain Greek-style nonfat yogurt
- For Serving

- 4 cups cooked whole-wheat egg noodles
- 4 teaspoons minced fresh parsley

Heat 2 teaspoons of the oil in a large skillet over medium-high heat. Add the beef and cook until browned on all sides, about 5 minutes. Transfer the meat with its juices to a plate.

Heat the remaining 2 teaspoons of oil in the skillet over medium-high heat. Add the onions and cook, stirring, until soft and translucent, about 3 minutes. Add the mushrooms and garlic and cook, stirring occasionally, until the mushrooms are soft and have released most of their water, about 5 minutes.

Return the beef and juices to the pan and stir to incorporate. Sprinkle with the flour and stir until well combined. Add the beef broth, wine, salt, and pepper and bring to a boil. Reduce the heat and simmer until the mixture thickens and reduces slightly, 5 minutes. Stir in the yogurt and cook for 1 minute more.

Spoon the mixture over the noodles and garnish with parsley. Serve alongside Green Beans and Grainy Mustard.

Makes 4 servings

Serving Size

1 cup noodles, 1 ½ cups beef-mushroom mixture, 1 teaspoon parsley, and about 16 green beans

Per Serving

Calories 560

Total Fat 15 g

Sat Fat 3.5 g Mono Fat 6.5 g Poly Fat 2.5 g

Protein 43 g

Carb 62 g

Fiber 7 g

Cholesterol 85 mg

Sodium 590 mg

Excellent Source of Copper, Fiber, Folate, Iron, Magnesium, Manganese, Niacin, Pantothenic Acid, Phosphorus, Potassium, Protein, Riboflavin, Selenium, Thiamin, Vitamin B6, Vitamin B12, Vitamin C, Vitamin K, Zinc.

Good Source of Calcium, Vitamin A.

FRESH GREEN BEANS AND GRAINY MUSTARD

Crisp green beans are just the right counterpoint to the rich stroganoff. Beads of tangy mustard dress them up deliciously with no effort at all.

- 1 pound fresh green beans, trimmed
- 2 teaspoons whole-grain mustard
- Salt and freshly ground black pepper to taste

Place the green beans in a steamer basket over a pot of boiling water. Cover and cook until crisp and tender, about 4 minutes. Drain the beans and transfer to a large serving bowl. Add the mustard and toss to coat. Season with salt and pepper and serve.

Makes 4 servings

Serving Size

About 16 green beans

EMERALD CHAO-BAO WITH BEEF

Whenever I stir fry (chao-bao) I crank up the dance tunes because the beat of making one is so fast and fun. The key is to get all your ingredients ready before you heat the pan so you can get into a groove. With this recipe the prep is a breeze thanks to vegetables, like snow peas, that require little or no chopping.

- 1 ¼ cup low-sodium soy sauce

- 1 ¼ cup mirin (Japanese rice wine) , or semisweet white wine (such as Riesling)
- ¼ cup orange juice
- `¼ cup water
- 2 tablespoons rice vinegar
- 1 ¼ teaspoon crushed red pepper flakes
- 2 tablespoons canola oil
- 8 ounces top round, London broil, or flank steak, thinly sliced
- 3 cloves garlic, minced
- 1 large bunch broccoli (1¼ pounds) , trimmed and cut into small florets
- 1 bunch asparagus (1¼ pound) , trimmed and sliced on diagonal into 2-inch pieces
- 2 cups (8 ounces) frozen shelled edamame
- 2 cups fresh snow peas (6 ounces)
- 1 ½ teaspoons cornstarch, dissolved in ¼ cup cold water
- 1 teaspoon toasted sesame oil
- 3 cups cooked brown rice

Combine the soy sauce, mirin or white wine, orange juice, water, rice vinegar, and red pepper flakes in a small bowl.

In a large wok or very large deep skillet, heat 1 tablespoon of the canola oil over medium-high heat. Add the beef and cook, stirring, until just browned, about 2 minutes. Transfer the beef to a plate. Heat the remaining tablespoon of canola oil in the same wok or skillet over medium heat. Add the garlic and cook, stirring, until fragrant, about 30 seconds. Add the broccoli, asparagus, edamame, and snow peas. Raise the heat to medium-high, and cook, stirring occasionally, until the vegetables are slightly softened, about 3 minutes.

Add the mirin-soy mixture and cook, stirring, until the vegetables are crisp-tender, about 4 minutes. Add the beef and dissolved cornstarch and stir to incorporate. Cook until the mixture thickens slightly and the beef is heated through, an additional 2 minutes. Drizzle with the sesame oil and serve over rice.

Makes 4 servings

Serving Size

2 cups stir-fry, 3 tablespoons sauce, ¾ cup cooked brown rice

Per Serving

Calories 540

Total Fat 15 g

Sat Fat 1.5 g Mono Fat 6 g Poly Fat 3 g

Protein 33 g

Carb 61 g

Fiber 12 g

Cholesterol 30 mg

Sodium 450 mg

Excellent Source of Fiber, Iron, Magnesium, Manganese, Niacin, Phosphorus, Protein, Selenium, Thiamin, Vitamin A, Vitamin B6, Vitamin C, Zinc.

Good Source of Calcium, Copper, Folate, Pantothenic Acid, Potassium, Riboflavin, Vitamin B12 .

STEAK CHIMICHURRI WITH GARLIC BRUSCHETTA AND TOMATOES

Chimichurri is a garlicky herb sauce, like pesto. It has been dubbed the ketchup of Argentina because they douse everything with it there vegetables, bread, eggs, chicken, fish-you name it. But it is an absolute must-have on grilled meat. After you try this you'll see why. The sauce takes minutes to make and you can prep it ahead so it's there when you need it.

For The Chimichurri Sauce

- 1/3 cup packed fresh cilantro
- 1/3 cup packed fresh Italian parsley
- 3 tablespoons olive oil
- large clove garlic
- tablespoon red wine vinegar
- 1 tablespoon water

- ¼ teaspoon crushed red pepper flakes
- ¼ teaspoon salt
- To Continue
- Cooking spray
- 1 ¼ pounds shoulder center steak (ranch steak) or top sirloin steak, about 1 ¼ inches thick
- ¼ teaspoon salt
- ¼ teaspoon freshly ground black pepper

Puree all the ingredients for the chimichurri sauce in the small bowl of a food processor until it reaches the consistency of a sauce. Transfer to a bowl. Chimichurri will keep in an airtight container in the refrigerator for up to 3 days.

To continue, spray a grill or grill pan with cooking spray and preheat over medium-high heat. Season the steak with the salt and pepper.

Cook the steak, turning once, for 5 minutes per side for medium rare, or to your desired degree of doneness. Allow the steak to sit for 5 minutes before slicing thinly.

Serve the steak with the chimichurri sauce, Grilled Garlic Bread, and Grilled Tomatoes.

Makes 4 servings

Serving Size

About 7 slices meat, 2 tablespoons sauce, 1 piece bread, and 2 tomato halves

Per Serving

Calories 470

Total Fat 25 g

Sat Fat 5 g Mono Fat 15 g Poly Fat 3.5 g

Protein 40 g

Carb 28 g

Fiber 6 g

Cholesterol 50 mg

Sodium 850 mg

Excellent Source of Fiber, Folate, Iron, Magnesium, Manganese, Niacin, Phosphorus, Potassium, Protein, Selenium, Thiamin, Vitamin A, Vitamin B6, Vitamin B12, Vitamin C, Vitamin K, Zinc.

Good Source of Calcium, Copper, Pantothenic Acid, Riboflavin.

BRUSCHETTA

Since you are firing up the grill for the steak, why not toast your bread too? The crisped bread acts as a gentle grater for fresh garlic, which takes it to the next level.

- 4 large slices crusty whole-grain country bread
- 1 tablespoon olive oil
- 1 clove garlic, cut in half
- ¼ teaspoon salt

Preheat a grill or grill pan over medium-high heat. Brush both sides of each slice of bread with oil. Grill until toasted and grill marks are formed, 2 to 3 minutes per side.

Rub both sides of the toasted bread vigorously with the garlic. Sprinkle with the salt and serve.

Makes 4 servings

Serving Size

1 piece

GRILLED TOMATOES

Grilling tomatoes transforms them by intensifying their flavor and bringing out their juiciness.

- 4 large ripe but firm tomatoes
- 1 tablespoon olive oil
- ¼ teaspoon salt

Cut the tomatoes in half crosswise and squeeze them gently to remove the seeds. Brush the cut side of each tomato with oil and season with salt. Preheat a grill or grill pan over medium-high heat. Place the tomatoes into the pan cut side down and grill until warm, softened, and browned on the cut side, but still retaining their shape, about 10 minutes.

Makes 4 servings

Serving Size

2 tomato halves

EXTRA BURGER WITH OLIVES AND CREAMY BROCCOLI SALAD

This burger is big, bold, and bursting at the seams with flavor. The combination of mouthwatering green olives, cumin, and parsley is just exotic enough to make it intriguing while still satisfying that all- American burger craving.

- 1 pound lean ground beef (at least 90% lean)
- ½ up coarsely chopped pitted green olives (2 ounces)
- 2 tablespoons finely chopped fresh Italian parsley
- ½ teaspoon ground cumin
- ¼ teaspoon freshly ground black pepper
- Cooking spray
- 4 whole-wheat burger buns
- 4 slices beefsteak tomato
- 4 green lettuce leaves
- ¼ red onion, sliced
- Ketchup, to taste

Combine the beef, olives, parsley, cumin, and pepper in a mixing bowl and mix until well incorporated. Shape into 4 burgers.

Spray a nonstick grill pan with cooking spray and preheat over medium-high heat or prepare an outdoor grill. Cook the burgers for about 4 minutes per side for medium, turning once. Place the burgers on the buns piled with tomato, lettuce, and onion slices. Serve the ketchup and Creamy Broccoli Salad alongside.

Makes 4 servings

Serving Size

1 burger with ¾ cup slaw

Per Serving

Calories 460

Total Fat 21 g

Sat Fat 3.5 g Mono Fat 8 g Poly Fat 9 g

Protein 34 g

Carb 36 g

Fiber 7 g

Cholesterol 65 mg

Sodium 920 mg

Excellent Source of Fiber, Folate, Iron, Magnesium, Manganese, Niacin, Phosphorus, Protein, Selenium, Thiamin, Vitamin A, Vitamin B12, Vitamin C, Vitamin K, Zinc.

Good Source of Calcium, Copper, Potassium, Riboflavin, Vitamin B6 .

CREAMY BROCCOLI SALAD

Like the burger, this salad is comfort food with flair. Here the twist is using crisp-tender, shredded broccoli stalks and a nutty crunch of sunflower seeds. You can maximize the easy factor by using a package of pre-shredded broccoli slaw mix, or shred your own to put the often wasted part of the broccoli to good use.

- ½ cup plain Greek-style nonfat yogurt
- 3 tablespoons mayonnaise
- 2 tablespoons fresh lemon juice
- 2 teaspoons honey
- ½ teaspoon salt
- ¼ teaspoon freshly ground black pepper
- 1 (12-ounce) package broccoli salad mix, or the stalks from 1 large head of broccoli and 1 large carrot
- ¼ cup shelled roasted sunflower seeds

In a large bowl, whisk together the yogurt, mayonnaise, lemon juice, honey, salt, and pepper. If using whole broccoli stalks and carrot, peel off the tough outer layer of the broccoli stalks and trim off ¼ inch from the bottom. Peel the carrot, then shred the broccoli stalks and carrot in a food processor with the shredder attachment. Add the shredded broccoli and carrots or broccoli salad mix to the dressing and toss to combine. Stir in the sunflower seeds and serve.

Makes 4 servings

Serving Size

¾ cup

EXOTIC PORK STIR-FRY

This dish is inspired by one of my favorite Chinese take-out orders. The pairing of succulent pork and sweet mango in a classic Asian sauce that balances savory-sweet-spicy and salty is absolutely mouthwatering.

- ¾ cup low-sodium chicken broth
- 2 teaspoons cornstarch
- 4 teaspoons canola oil
- pound lean pork tenderloin, thinly sliced

- 1 medium red onion, sliced
- 1 large red bell pepper, seeded and chopped
- tablespoons minced peeled fresh ginger
- cloves garlic, sliced
- ¾ pound snow peas
- ¼ cup Chinese cooking wine or dry sherry
- tablespoons low-sodium soy sauce
- 1 ¼ teaspoons Chinese five-spice powder
- ½ teaspoon crushed red pepper flakes
- 1 large firm but ripe mango, peeled, pitted, and cut into chunks
- 3 cups cooked brown rice

In a small bowl, whisk together the chicken broth and cornstarch until the cornstarch is dissolved.

Heat 2 teaspoons of the oil in a wok or very large skillet over medium-high heat. Add the pork and cook, stirring occasionally, until just cooked through, about 4 minutes. Transfer the meat to a plate.

Heat the remaining 2 teaspoons of oil in the same wok or skillet. Add the onions, peppers, ginger, and garlic and cook, stirring, until the vegetables are softened, about 3 minutes. Add the snow peas, cornstarch-broth mixture, wine or sherry, soy sauce, Chinese five-spice powder, and red pepper flakes and toss to combine. Cook until the peas are crisp-tender and the sauce thickens slightly, about 3 minutes. Return the pork to the wok. Add the mango and heat through, about 2 minutes more. Serve over the rice.

Makes 4 servings

Serving Size

2 cups stir-fry plus ¾ cup cooked brown rice

Per Serving

Calories 470

Total Fat 9 g

Sat Fat 1.5 g Mono Fat 4.5 g Poly Fat 2.5 g

Protein 33 g

Carb 56 g

Fiber 7 g

Cholesterol 75 mg

Sodium 470 mg

Excellent Source of Fiber, Iron, Magnesium, Manganese, Niacin, Pantothenic Acid, Phosphorus, Potassium, Protein, Riboflavin, Selenium, Thiamin, Vitamin A, Vitamin B6, Vitamin C, Zinc.

Good Source of Copper, Folate, Vitamin B12.

STEAK PORK PICCATA WITH SPINACH AND MASHED POTATOES WITH GARLIC

This dish showcases one of my everyday favorite ways to cook- browning meat in a skillet, then creating a sauce using the pan scrapings for maximum flavor. It is quick and simple, and you get your protein and sauce in one pan. Here the meat is meltingly tender pork tenderloin and the sauce is a delectable lemony wine reduction enhanced with briny capers.

- ¼ cup all-purpose flour
- ¾ teaspoon salt
- ¾ teaspoon freshly ground black pepper
- 1 ¼ pounds pork tenderloin, sliced crosswise into ¼ -inch-thick medallions
- 2 tablespoons olive oil
- 3 cloves garlic, minced
- 1 cup dry white wine
- 1 cup low-sodium chicken broth
- 3 tablespoons fresh lemon juice
- 2 tablespoons drained capers
- 2 tablespoons chopped parsley

Combine the flour and VI teaspoon each of salt and pepper in a sealable plastic bag. Place the pork medallions in the bag and shake until well-coated.

Heat 1 tablespoon of the oil in a large skillet (not nonstick) over medium-high heat. Working in 2 batches, cook the pork until it is browned on both sides, 1 to 2 minutes per side. Transfer the meat to a plate.

Add the garlic to the same skillet, then immediately add the wine and cook over medium-high heat. As the wine reduces, stir to dissolve the small bits and juices remaining in the pan from the meat. Cook until the wine is reduced by about half, 4 to 5 minutes.

Add the chicken broth, lemon juice, capers, and remaining salt and pepper and cook until the mixture has reduced slightly, an additional 3 to 4 minutes. Return the medallions to the skillet along with the remaining tablespoon of oil and heat until the sauce thickens and the meat is cooked to medium doneness, about 3 minutes.

Serve over the Express "Steamed" Spinach and Garlic Mashed Potatoes, and top with the parsley.

Makes 4 servings

Serving Size

5 to 6 medallions, 2 tablespoons sauce, ¼ cup spinach, and ¾ cup mashed potatoes

Per Serving

Calories 470

Total Fat 15 g

Sat Fat 2.5 g Mono Fat 9.5 g Poly Fat 2 g

Protein 37 g

Carb 35 g

Fiber 5g

Cholesterol 90 mg

Sodium 880 mg

Excellent Source of Copper, Folate, Iron, Magnesium, Manganese, Niacin, Phosphorus, Potassium, Protein, Riboflavin, Selenium, Thiamin, Vitamin A, Vitamin B6, Vitamin C, Vitamin K, Zinc.

Good Source of Fiber, Pantothenic Acid, Vitamin B12.

EXPRESS " STEAMED " SPINACH

Steamed spinach is a fresh, colorful, subtly flavored side that is heavenly with the lemony Pork Piccata sauce. When you make the spinach this way, you barely have to lift a finger.

- 5 ounces pre-washed baby spinach leaves

Place the spinach in a large microwave-safe bowl and cover tightly. Microwave on high for 90 seconds.

Makes 4 servings

Serving Size

¼ cup

MASHED POTATOES WITH GARLIC

What better bed for pork with lemon and wine sauce than garlicky mashed potatoes? This mash owes its luxurious texture to the natural creaminess of Yukon Gold potatoes and a touch of olive oil. At first glance 4 cloves of garlic may seem like a lot, but the garlic mellows as it steams with the potatoes, so when they are mashed together you get just the right garlic infusion.

- 1 ¼ pounds Yukon Gold potatoes, left unpeeled and cut into 1-inch pieces
- 4 large cloves garlic, peeled and quartered
- ½ cup low-sodium chicken broth
- 1 tablespoon olive oil
- ½ teaspoon salt

Place the potatoes and garlic in a steamer basket fitted over a large pot of boiling water. Cover and steam until the potatoes are knife-tender, 12 to 15 minutes. Warm the chicken broth in a small saucepan on the stove or in a glass container in the microwave. Remove the steamer basket and drain the water from the large pot. Transfer the potatoes and garlic to the pot, add the oil, salt, and broth, and mash until smooth.

Makes 4 servings

Serving Size

¾ cup

MEDITERRANEAN GLAZED PORK WITH MAPLE SQUASH PUREE AND SPINACH-GREEN

The simplicity of this recipe belies its complex flavors-spicy, sweet, smoky, and citrus-all lighting up succulent grilled pork chops.

- 2 tablespoons pure maple syrup
- 2 tablespoons thawed frozen orange juice concentrate
- 1 teaspoon finely chopped, seeded, canned chipotle chile plus ½ teaspoon adobo sauce it comes in
- Cooking spray
- 4 ¾ -inch-thick center cut, bone-in pork loin chops (about 8 ounces each)
- ½ teaspoon salt

In a small bowl, combine the maple syrup, orange juice concentrate, and chipotle.

Spray a nonstick grill pan or grill with cooking spray and preheat over medium-high heat.

Sprinkle both sides of the chops with the salt. Brush one side of the chops generously with the maple-orange glaze. Place the chops on the grill pan, glazed-side down. Brush the other side with glaze. Cook over medium-high heat until cooked through but with a slight blush in the center, 3 to 4 minutes per side.

Serve with the Maple Squash Puree and Spinach-Green Apple Salad.

Makes 4 servings

Serving Size

1 pork chop, 2/3 cup squash puree, and 2 cups salad

Per Serving

Calories 570

Total Fat 24 g

Sat Fat 6 g Mono Fat 10 g Poly Fat 6 g

Protein 37 g

Carb 52 g

Fiber 5 g

Cholesterol 100 mg

Sodium 550 mg

Excellent Source of Copper, Folate, Iron, Magnesium, Manganese, Niacin, Phosphorus, Potassium, Protein, Riboflavin, Selenium, Thiamin, Vitamin A, Vitamin B6, Vitamin C, Zinc.

Good Source of Calcium, Fiber, Pantothenic Acid, Vitamin B12.

Tip:

Chop the leftover chipotle peppers and divide them, along with the adobo sauce, among three or four small sealable plastic bags, then store them in the freezer.

MAPLE SQUASH PUREE

Brilliant orange squash is a vegetable everyone in the family loves, especially when you sweeten the deal with maple syrup. A dab of butter works wonders to make it ultra rich and creamy. You can also make this slow-food style with fresh roasted squash, but frozen works perfectly when time is tight.

- 2 (12-ounce) packages frozen cooked butternut squash or winter squash
- 1/3 cup water
- 2 tablespoons pure maple syrup
- 1 ½ tablespoon butter

Salt to taste

Put the frozen squash and water into a large saucepan. Cover and cook over medium heat, stirring frequently, until the squash is thawed, about 10 minutes. Whisk in the maple syrup and butter and season with salt.

Makes 4 servings

Serving Size

2/3 cup

SPINACH-GREEN

This salad is just as easy as your run-of-the-mill lettuce, tomato, and cucumber salad, but oh, so much more interesting. It is a gorgeous balance of texture, color, and taste and has a real autumnal feel.

- 2-3 tablespoons extra-virgin olive oil
- 1 tablespoon cider vinegar
- 1 teaspoon Dijon mustard
- Salt and freshly ground black pepper to taste
- ounces baby spinach leaves (about 5 cups lightly packed)
- 2 Granny Smith apple
- 1/3 cup walnut pieces, toasted in a dry skillet over medium-high heat until fragrant, about 2 minutes

In a small bowl, whisk together the oil, vinegar, and mustard. Season with salt and pepper. In a large bowl, toss the spinach with the dressing until evenly coated, then divide the spinach among 4 serving plates.

Core the apple and slice it into matchsticks. Sprinkle a quarter of the apple pieces on top of each salad. Follow with the walnut pieces.

Serve immediately.

Makes 4 servings

Serving Size

2 cups

CHICKEN-MUSHROOM TORTILLA

This recipe upgrades tortilla from the appetizer menu to a first-class dinner entree. It has everything you need-protein, vegetables, and whole grain, all brought together quick as can be with oozy melted cheddar.

- 1 tablespoon canola oil
- 1 large onion, chopped
- 8 ounces white button mushrooms, coarsely chopped (about 3 cups)
- 3 cloves garlic, minced
- 2 cups cooked diced skinless boneless chicken breast (1 breast half)
- 1 teaspoon ground cumin
- 1 teaspoon chili powder
- 1 teaspoon dried oregano
- 2 cups baby spinach leaves, coarsely chopped
- ½ teaspoon salt
- ¼ teaspoon freshly ground black pepper
- 4 10-inch whole-wheat-flour tortillas
- 1 cup shredded sharp cheddar cheese (4 ounces)
- ½ cup salsa
- ¼ cup reduced-fat sour cream

Heat the oil in a large skillet over medium heat. Add the onions and mushrooms and cook, stirring occasionally, until the mushroom water has evaporated and they begin to brown, 5 to 7 minutes. Add the garlic and cook, stirring, for 1 minute more. Add the chicken, cumin, chili powder, and oregano and stir until all the spices are incorporated. Stir in the spinach, salt, and pepper and cook until the spinach is wilted, about 2 minutes.

Lay the tortillas on a flat surface. Sprinkle half of each tortilla with 2 tablespoons of shredded cheese. Spoon ½ of the chicken mixture on top of the cheese on each tortilla, then top each with 2 more tablespoons of cheese and fold the tortillas over into half-moons, pressing down lightly to seal them closed.

Spray a large nonstick skillet with cooking spray and preheat over medium heat. Place 2 quesadillas in the pan and cook, turning once, until lightly browned and the cheese is melted, about 3 minutes per side. Repeat with the remaining quesadillas. Slice each quesadilla in half. Serve with the salsa and sour cream.

Makes 4 servings

Serving Size

2 quesadilla pieces, 2 tablespoons salsa, and 1 tablespoon sour cream

Per Serving

Calories 440

Total Fat 19 g

Sat Fat 8 g Mono Fat 5 g Poly Fat 1. 5 g

Protein 23 g

Carb 44 g

Fiber 8 g

Cholesterol 55 mg

Sodium 1000 mg

Excellent Source of Calcium, Fiber, Manganese, Niacin, Phosphorus, Protein, Riboflavin, Selenium.

Good Source of Copper, Pantothenic Acid, Potassium, Vitamin A, Vitamin B6, Vitamin C, Vitamin K, Zinc.

BARBECUE CHICKEN SANDWICHES WITH CLASSIC COLESLAW

Rotisserie chicken is a reliable fallback, but as is, it can be just plain boring. In less than 30 minutes, this recipe turns that chicken into a fabulous sandwich with a tangy barbecue sauce that tastes like you have been cooking all day.

- tablespoon canola oil
- 1 large onion, chopped
- cloves garlic, minced
- 1 (14-ounce) can low-sodium tomato sauce
- ½ cup water
- 1/3 cup cider vinegar
- 5 tablespoons unsulfured molasses
- ¼ cup tomato paste
- ½ teaspoon liquid smoke
- ¼ teaspoon freshly ground black pepper
- 1 whole rotisserie chicken
- 6 whole-wheat hamburger buns
- 6 large green lettuce leaves

Heat the oil in a large skillet over medium heat. Add the onions and cook, stirring, until soft and translucent, about 5 minutes. Add the garlic and cook, stirring, for 1 minute more. Add the tomato sauce, water, vinegar, molasses, tomato paste, liquid smoke, and pepper and bring to a boil. Reduce the heat to medium-low and simmer for 15 minutes.

Meanwhile, take the meat off the chicken, discarding the skin and bones, and shred the meat into thin strips. Add the chicken to the sauce in the pan, return to a simmer, and cook for an additional 10 minutes.

Split the buns. Place a leaf of lettuce on each, then pile ⅔ cup of the chicken mixture onto the buns. Serve with the Classic Coleslaw.

Makes 6 servings

Serving Size

1 sandwich and 2/3 cup coleslaw

Per Serving

Calories 550

Total Fat 19 g

Sat Fat 3.5 g Mono Fat 6.5 g Poly Fat 7.5 g

Protein 39 g

Carb 57 g

Fiber 7 g

Cholesterol 95 mg

Sodium 680 mg

Excellent Source of Copper, Fiber, Iron, Magnesium, Manganese, Niacin, Phosphorus, Potassium, Protein, Selenium, Vitamin A, Vitamin B6, Vitamin C, Zinc.

Good Source of Calcium, Pantothenic Acid, Riboflavin, Thiamin, Vitamin K.

CLASSIC COLESLAW

What goes better with BBQ than classic creamy coleslaw? Well, here you have it. Lickety split.

- ½ cup plain Greek-style nonfat yogurt
- ¼ cup mayonnaise
- ¼ cup cider vinegar
- 1 tablespoon honey
- ½ teaspoon salt
- ¼ teaspoon freshly ground black pepper
- (1 6-ounce) bag shredded coleslaw mix or ½ head of green cabbage and 3 large carrots, peeled and shredded
- 2 teaspoons caraway seeds (optional)

In a large bowl, whisk together the yogurt, mayonnaise, vinegar, honey, salt, and pepper. Add the coleslaw mix or the shredded cabbage and carrots, and the caraway seeds, if using, and toss to coat.

Makes 6 servings

Serving Size

2/3 cup

TASTY PEACH CHICKEN

This dish transforms basic chicken breast into a fantastic meal with a teriyaki-like sauce chock-full of peaches that give it an absolutely delightful fruity infusion.

- ¼ cup orange juice
- 2 tablespoons brown sugar
- 2 tablespoons low-sodium soy sauce
- 2 tablespoons rice vinegar
- 2 tablespoon canola oil
- 4 skinless boneless chicken breasts (about 1 ¼ pounds total)
- ½ teaspoon salt
- ¼ teaspoon freshly ground black pepper
- 1 teaspoon grated peeled fresh ginger
- 2 cloves garlic, minced
- ½ cup low-sodium chicken broth
- 4 large firm but ripe peaches, sliced into ¼ -inch slices, or two 10- ounce packages frozen peaches (about 4 ½ cups)
- 3 cups cooked brown rice
- 2 tablespoons sliced almonds, toasted in a dry skillet over medium- high heat for 2 minutes
- 3 cups steamed broccoli spears

In a small bowl, whisk together the orange juice, brown sugar, soy sauce, and rice vinegar until the sugar is dissolved.

Heat 1 tablespoon of the oil in a large skillet over medium-high heat. Season the chicken on both sides with the salt and pepper. Add to the skillet and cook until browned, about 2 minutes per side. Transfer the chicken to a plate.

Heat the remaining tablespoon of oil in the same skillet, then add the ginger and garlic and cook, stirring, for 30 seconds. Add the chicken broth, soy sauce mixture, and peaches; turn the heat up to high and cook, uncovered, stirring occasionally, until the sauce is slightly thickened and the peaches soften, about 6 minutes. Add the chicken back to the pan, reduce the heat to medium-low, cover, and cook until the chicken is cooked through, about 5 minutes.

Serve the chicken over the rice, topped with the sauce and sprinkled with the toasted almonds. Place a few broccoli spears alongside.

Makes 4 servings

Serving Size

1 piece chicken, 2/3 cup sauce, ½ tablespoon almonds, ¾ cup broccoli, and ¾ cup cooked brown rice

Per Serving

Calories 530

Total Fat 14 g

Sat Fat 2 g Mono Fat 7 g Poly Fat 4 g

Protein 38 g

Carb 62 g

Fiber 7 g

Cholesterol 80 mg

Sodium 580 mg

Excellent Source of Fiber, Magnesium, Manganese, Niacin, Pantothenic Acid, Phosphorus, Potassium, Protein, Selenium, Vitamin A, Vitamin B6, Vitamin C.

Good Source of Copper, Folate, Iron, Riboflavin, Thiamin, Vitamin K, Zinc.

CHICKEN WITH TOMATO-CORN MIX

This recipe evokes a summer day. It's packed with seasonal bounty- tomatoes, corn, scallions, and fresh herbs-enlivened with a splash of lime, and enriched with buttery avocado slices. Whip it up in the summer (without breaking a sweat!) after a trip to the farm stand, or anytime you just need a taste of a sun-soaked season.

- 1 ¼ pounds thin-cut skinless boneless chicken breasts
- ¼ teaspoon salt, plus more to taste
- ¼ teaspoon freshly ground black pepper, plus more to taste
- 4 teaspoons olive oil
- 4 scallions, white and green separated
- 2 cloves garlic, minced
- 2 pints grape tomatoes, halved
- 2 cups corn kernels (from 4 ears fresh uncooked corn or frozen)
- 1 ripe avocado, pitted, peeled, sliced
- 3 tablespoons fresh lime juice
- 3 tablespoons chopped fresh cilantro

Season the chicken with ¼ teaspoon each of salt and pepper. Heat 2 teaspoons of the oil in a large nonstick skillet over medium-high heat. Add the chicken to the pan and cook until the chicken is browned and cooked through, about 3 minutes per side. Transfer the chicken to a plate.

Add the remaining 2 teaspoons of oil to the pan and heat over medium-high heat. Add the scallion whites and cook, stirring, for 1 minute. Add the garlic and cook, stirring, for 30 seconds more. Add the tomatoes and corn to the pan and cook until they are softened but still retain their shape, about 3 minutes. Stir in the scallion greens and season with salt and pepper to taste.

Place about a cup of the vegetable mixture on each plate. Top with a piece of chicken breast and slices of avocado. Sprinkle with lime juice and cilantro and serve.

Makes 4 servings

Serving Size

1 cup vegetables, 1 piece chicken breast, and ¼ avocado

Per Serving

Calories 400

Total Fat 16 g

Sat Fat 3 g Mono Fat 10 g Poly Fat 3 g

Protein 34 g

Carb 32 g

Fiber 8 g

Cholesterol 80 mg

Sodium 230 mg

Excellent Source of Fiber, Folate, Magnesium, Manganese, Niacin, Phosphorus, Potassium, Protein, Selenium, Thiamin, Vitamin A, Vitamin B6, Vitamin C, Vitamin K.

Good Source of Copper, Iron, Pantothenic Acid, Riboflavin, Zinc.

PANZANELLA WITH SPICY CHICKEN SAUSAGE

The first time I ever had panzanella (tomato and bread salad) I was sitting in the garden of an Italian restaurant on a warm, crystal clear day in New York. The dish was a revelation-so simple yet so satisfying. One bite of this dish brings me right back there, and it is practically as relaxing to make.

- 8 medium ripe tomatoes, cut into wedges (about 1 ½ pounds)
- 1 small English cucumber, cut into half moons
- ½ medium red onion, thinly sliced into half moons
- 3 tablespoons olive oil
- 1 tablespoon red wine vinegar
- ½ teaspoon salt
- ¼ teaspoon freshly ground black pepper
- Chilli powder
- 1 small whole-grain baguette or other crusty bread (preferably day-old; about 8 ounces), cut into ¾-inch chunks
- 1/3 cup basil leaves, coarsely chopped
- 1 (12-ounce) package Italian-style pre-cooked chicken sausage

In a large bowl, toss together the tomatoes, cucumber, onion, oil, vinegar, salt, chilli powder and pepper. Add the bread chunks and basil and toss well so all the bread is well moistened.

Preheat a grill or grill pan over medium-high heat. Add the sausage and cook, turning once or twice, until warmed through and grill marks are formed, about 8 minutes. Serve the sausage, whole, alongside the panzanella.

Makes 4 servings

Serving Size

2 ½ cups panzanella and 1 sausage

Per Serving

Calories 510

Total Fat 25 g

Sat Fat 5 g Mono Fat 8 g Poly Fat 3 g

Protein 37 g

Carb 40 g

Fiber 10 g

Cholesterol 11 0 mg

Sodium 540 mg

Excellent Source of Fiber, Folate, Manganese, Potassium, Protein, Selenium, Vitamin A, Vitamin C, Vitamin K.

Good Source of Copper, Iron, Magnesium, Niacin, Phosphorus, Thiamin, Vitamin B6.

Did You Know?

Chicken and turkey sausage contain 1/3 the calories and 1/3 the fat of regular pork sausage.

FLAKY FLOUNDER WITH ALMOND TOPPING, SAFFRON RICE, AND CITRUS BROCCOLINI

The almonds toast and become golden brown as the fish cooks, crowning the mild, flaky flounder with delightful richness and crunch. It's amazing how much taste and appeal you get from such a simple topping.

- Cooking spray
- 4 (6-ounce) flounder fillets
- ½ cup sliced almonds, finely chopped
- 1 tablespoon plus 1 teaspoon fresh thyme, chopped, or 1 ½ teaspoons dried
- ½ teaspoon finely grated lemon zest
- ½ teaspoon salt
- ½ teaspoon freshly ground black pepper
- 1/8 teaspoon cayenne pepper
- 3 tablespoons fresh lemon juice

Preheat the oven to 400°F. Spray a baking sheet with cooking spray. Rinse and pat dry the fish fillets and lay them on the baking sheet.

In a small bowl, combine the almonds, thyme, lemon zest, salt, black pepper, and cayenne pepper. Sprinkle V! of the nut mixture onto each fillet and gently press into the surface. Bake for 10 minutes, then broil on high until the fish flakes easily and the nuts are golden brown, about 2 minutes. Drizzle with the lemon juice and serve with the Citrus Broccolini and Saffron Rice.

Makes 4 servings

Serving Size

1 fish fillet, ¾ cup rice, and 1 cup broccolini

Per Serving

Calories 500

Total Fat 12 g

Sat Fat 1.5 g Mono Fat 7 g Poly Fat 3 g

Protein 45 g

Carb 52 g

Fiber 4 g

Cholesterol 80 mg

Sodium 940 mg

Excellent Source of Folate, Iron, Magnesium, Manganese, Niacin, Phosphorus, Potassium, Protein, Selenium, Thiamin, Vitamin A, Vitamin B6, Vitamin B12, Vitamin C, Vitamin D, Calcium, Fiber, Zinc.

SAFFRON RICE

This is one place I prefer to use white rice because it really lets the brilliant orange-yellow color and distinctive taste of the saffron come through. Cooking the rice in chicken broth makes it extra-rich and flavorful. It makes a tasty and gorgeous background for the nutty fish and lemony broccolini.

- 2 cups low-sodium chicken broth
- Generous pinch of saffron threads
- 1 cup long-grain white rice
- ½ teaspoon salt

Put the broth and saffron into a medium pot and bring to a boil. Stir in the rice and salt, then cover and simmer over low heat until all the water is absorbed, about 20 minutes.

Makes 4 servings

Serving Size

¾ cup

CITRUS BROCCOLINI

Broccolini is a cross between regular broccoli and Chinese broccoli and has longer, more tender stems and a slightly sweeter taste than regular broccoli. Here it gets the lemon-olive oil treatment, which makes it lip-smackingly delicious.

- 1 pound broccolini
- 1 tablespoon fresh lemon juice
- 1 tablespoon olive oil
- 2 teaspoon finely grated lemon zest
- ¼ teaspoon salt

Pinch of freshly ground black pepper

Wash and trim the broccolini. Place it in a steamer basket fitted over a pot of boiling water. Cover and steam until it is crisp yet tender, about 5 minutes. Drain. In a large bowl, whisk together the lemon juice, oil, zest, salt, and pepper. Add the broccolini to the bowl and toss to coat.

Makes 4 servings

Serving Size

1 cup

SHRIMP WITH GARLIC AND BASIL

This recipe wins hands down in the easy, fast, and delicious category. It takes just 6 minutes to cook, you hardly have to chop a thing, and you get a plateful of garlicky shrimp and warm plump tomatoes in a lovely light sauce.

- 2 tablespoons olive oil
- 1 ½ pounds large shrimp (20 to 25 per pound), peeled and deveined
- 3 garlic cloves, minced
- 1/8 teaspoon crushed red pepper flakes, or more to taste
- ¾ cup dry white wine
- 1 ½ cups grape tomatoes, halved
- ¼ cup finely chopped fresh basil
- Salt and freshly ground black pepper, to taste
- 3 cups cooked orzo pasta, preferably whole wheat

Heat the oil in a large heavy skillet over medium-high heat until hot but not smoking, then add the shrimp and cook, turning over once, until just cooked through, about 2 minutes. Transfer with a slotted spoon to a large bowl.

Add the garlic and red pepper flakes to the oil remaining in the skillet and cook until fragrant, about 30 seconds. Add the wine and cook over high heat, stirring occasionally, for 3 minutes. Stir in the tomatoes and basil and season the sauce with salt and pepper. Return the shrimp to the pan and cook just until heated through. Serve with the orzo.

Makes 4 servings

Serving Size

1 cup shrimp mixture and ¾ cup orzo

Per Serving

Calories 390

Total Fat 10 g

Sat Fat 1.5 g

Mono Fat 5.5 g Poly Fat 2 g

Protein 36 g

Carb 35 g

Fiber 4 g

Cholesterol 215 mg

Sodium 490 mg

Excellent Source of Copper, Iron, Magnesium, Manganese, Niacin, Phosphorus, Protein, Selenium, Vitamin B12, Vitamin D, Vitamin K.

Good Source of Calcium, Fiber, Potassium, Thiamin, Vitamin A, Vitamin B6, Vitamin C, Zinc.

SALMON WITH CHICKPEA RAGU AND LEMON

Hooray for the versatile chickpea! It is happily eaten mashed or whole, hot or cold, and it is at home around the world, in the Americas, the Mediterranean, or the Middle East. Here it finds itself in a flavorful herbed vegetable stew as a satisfying bed for buttery salmon.

- 1 tablespoon olive oil
- 1 small onion, chopped
- 1 large carrot, peeled and diced
- 1 large zucchini, diced
- 2 cloves garlic, minced
- 2 tablespoons tomato paste
- 4 cups low-sodium chicken broth
- 1 (1 5.5-ounce) can chickpeas (preferably low-sodium) , drained and rinsed
- 1 cup basil leaves, sliced into ribbons, plus more f or garnish
- ½ teaspoon salt
- ½ lemon
- ½ teaspoon freshly ground black pepper
- 4 (6-ounce) skinless salmon fillets

Heat the oil in a large skillet over medium-high heat, add the onion, and cook until soft and translucent, about 3 minutes. Add the carrot, zucchini, and garlic and cook, stirring, until the carrots are firm- tender, 4 to 5 minutes. Add the tomato paste, stirring to incorporate completely. Add the chicken broth and chickpeas and bring to a boil. Reduce the heat to low and cook, covered, until the liquid thickens slightly, 8 to 10 minutes.

Remove the skillet from the heat, add 1 cup of the basil and ¼ teaspoon each of salt and pepper, and stir to incorporate. Cover to keep warm while you cook the salmon.

Preheat the broiler. Season the salmon with the remaining ¼ teaspoon each of salt and pepper. Broil the salmon for 8 to 10 minutes per inch thickness, turning once.

To serve, spoon 1 ½ cups of the chickpea ragu into a shallow bowl or rimmed plate. Top with a fillet of salmon, garnish with ribbons of basil and squeeze the lemon over it .

Makes 4 servings

Serving Size

1 ½ cups chickpea ragu and 1 salmon fillet

Per Serving

Calories 470

Total Fat 17 g

Sat Fat 2.5 g Mono Fat 7 Poly Fat 5 g

Protein 47 g

Carb 32 g

Fiber 6 g

Cholesterol 95 mg

Sodium 550 mg

Excellent Source of Copper, Fiber, Iron, Magnesium, Niacin, Pantothenic Acid, Phosphorus, Potassium, Protein, Riboflavin, Selenium, Thiamin, Vitamin A, Vitamin B6, Vitamin B12, Vitamin C, Vitamin 0, Vitamin K.

Good Source of Calcium, Folate, Manganese, Zinc.

PROSCIUTTO CRUDO-WRAPPED SALMON WITH PESTO POTATOES AND GREEN BEANS

Talk about fast! You barely need twenty minutes to make this unbelievably delicious and impressive-looking dish. The decadent pairing of flaky rich cod and cured Italian ham give new meaning to surf-and-turf.

- 4 (6-ounce) salmon fillets
- ¼ teaspoon salt
- ¼ teaspoon freshly ground black pepper 2 ounces thinly sliced prosciutto
- Cooking spray

Season the fish on both sides with the salt and pepper. Wrap one wide or two thin slices of prosciutto around each piece of salmon. Spray a large nonstick skillet with cooking spray and preheat it over medium-high heat. Add the fish fillets and cook until the prosciutto is crisp and the fish is cooked through, 3 to 4 minutes per side. Serve with the Pesto Potatoes and Green Beans

Makes 4 servings

Serving Size

1 prosciutto-wrapped fillet and 1 ¾ cups potatoes and green beans

Per Serving

Calories 430

Total Fat 8 g

Sat Fat 1.5 g Mono Fat 0 g Poly Fat 0.5 g

Protein 43g

Carb 44 g

Fiber 7 g

Cholesterol 90 mg

Sodium 750 mg

Excellent Source of Copper, Fiber, Folate, Magnesium, Manganese, Niacin, Phosphorus, Potassium, Protein, Selenium, Thiamin, Vitamin A, Vitamin B6, Vitamin B12, Vitamin C, Vitamin K.

Good Source of Calcium, Iron, Riboflavin, Vitamin D, Zinc.

Did You Know?

The fat found in fish-called omega-3-can help protect your heart, alleviate symptoms of arthritis, keep your brain healthy, and improve your mood. It's also a beauty must-key for maintaining healthy, dewy skin.

PESTO POTATOES AND GREEN BEANS

This dish is a real two-for-one deal where you get both sides in one super-simple dish. It's a warm potato and green bean salad dressed in aromatic basil pesto that's a great match for the Prosciutto-Wrapped Salmon. It is also excellent at room temperature the next day if you are lucky enough to have leftovers.

- 1 pounds red new potatoes, cut into 1-inch chunks
- 2 pound green beans, trimmed and cut into l-inch pieces
- 3 tablespoons store-bought basil pesto

Salt and freshly ground black pepper to taste

Place the potatoes in a large steamer basket fitted over a pot of boiling water. Cover and steam for 6 minutes. Add the green beans to the potatoes in the steamer and continue to cook, covered, for another 4 minutes. Transfer the vegetables to a large serving bowl. Add the pesto and stir to coat evenly. Season with salt and pepper and serve.

Makes 4 servings

Serving Size

1 ¾ cups

MUSSELS PROVENCAL WITH TRIO SALAD

Mussels are an everyday food in France and Belgium, and when you try this recipe you'll see why. They are fast and effortless to make, fun to eat, and utterly delicious. They are an upscale treat for grown-ups, but kids love them too because they get to eat out of a shell. This recipe makes two servings because that's all that fits in a typical pot. If you want to serve four, just double the recipe and use two pots or a jumbo stock pot.

- 2 teaspoons olive oil
- 2 shallots, finely chopped (about ½ cup)
- 2 cloves garlic, very thinly sliced
- 1 teaspoon chopped fresh thyme, or ½ teaspoon dried
- 1 (15-ounce) can whole tomatoes, drained and chopped
- 1 tablespoon tomato paste
- 1/3 cup dry white wine
- 2 pounds cultivated mussels, rinsed and debearded
- 4 slices whole-wheat baguette

In a large pot, heat the oil over medium heat. Add the shallots and cook, stirring occasionally, until softened, 3 to 5 minutes. Add the garlic and thyme and cook, stirring, until fragrant, 1 to 2 minutes longer. Stir in the canned tomatoes and tomato paste and simmer, partially covered, for 10 minutes.

Add the wine and bring to a boil over high heat. Add the mussels, cover, and cook just until the mussels have opened, about 3 minutes; discard any mussels that have not opened. Transfer the mussels and sauce to individual serving bowls and serve with the bread and the salad on the side.

Makes 2 servings

Serving Size

About 20 mussels, 2 bread slices, and 1 ½ cups salad

Per Serving

Calories 580

Total Fat 24 g

Sat Fat 4 g Mono Fat 14 g Poly Fat 3 g

Protein 34 g

Carb 55 g

Fiber 10 g

Cholesterol 50 mg

Sodium 1410 mg

Excellent Source of Calcium, Copper, Fiber, Folate, Iron, Magnesium, Manganese, Niacin, Pantothenic Acid, Phosphorus, Potassium, Protein, Riboflavin, Selenium, Thiamin, Vitamin A, Vitamin B6, Vitamin B12, Vitamin C, Vitamin K, Zinc.

TRIO SALAD

The tried and true trio of bacon, lettuce, and tomato make a scrumptious side for the mussels. Something magical happens when you serve shellfish with pork, especially when the pork has a deep smokiness, like the lean Canadian bacon used here.

- Cooking spray
- 4 slices Canadian bacon (4 ounces), diced
- 1 tablespoon plus 2 teaspoons olive oil
- 2 teaspoons red wine vinegar
- 1/8 teaspoon salt
- Pinch of freshly ground black pepper
- 1 medium head frisee lettuce (about 3 cups lightly packed), torn
- 3 medium tomatoes, seeded and diced

Spray a nonstick skillet with cooking spray and heat over medium- high heat. Add the Canadian bacon and cook, stirring occasionally, until the bacon is crisp, about 5 minutes. Remove from the heat.

In a large bowl, whisk together the oil, vinegar, salt, and pepper. Add the frisee and toss until well coated. Divide the frisee between 2 serving plates. Top with the diced tomatoes and crisped bacon and serve.

Makes 2 servings

Serving Size

1 ½ cups

SESAME SHRIMP WITH RICE AND CABBAGE

This dish is a ten-minute meal in a bowl that gives you all the full- flavor satisfaction of fried rice without loads of grease and salt. Make sure you use very cold cooked rice (hello leftover Chinese food) , or you will wind up with a sticky mess.

- 1 tablespoon canola oil
- 1 pound peeled cleaned small shrimp
- 4 scallions (white and green parts) , thinly sliced
- 1 tablespoon grated peeled fresh ginger
- 5 Cups thinly sliced green cabbage, cut crosswise into 3-inch pieces
- 1 tablespoon toasted sesame oil
- 4 cups very cold cooked brown rice
- 3 tablespoons low-sodium soy sauce
- 2 tablespoons sesame seeds, toasted in a dry skillet over medium- high heat for about 1 minute, until golden

Heat the oil in a very large nonstick skillet or wok over high heat. Add the shrimp, scallions, and ginger and cook, stirring frequently, until the shrimp turn pink, about   1 ½ minutes.   Add the   cabbage and continue cooking, stirring occasionally, until it begins to soften but is still somewhat crisp, about 2 minutes more. Transfer the shrimp- cabbage mixture to a bowl.

Heat the sesame oil in the same skillet or wok over medium-high heat. Add the rice and cook, stirring frequently, until heated through, about 3 minutes. Add the shrimp-cabbage mixture back to the skillet, stir in the soy sauce and sesame seeds, and serve.

Makes 4 servings

Serving Size

2 cups

Per Serving

Calories 470

Total Fat 12 g Sat Fat 1.5 g

Mono Fat 4.5 g Poly Fat 3.5 g

Protein 34 g

Carb 55 g

Fiber 8 g

Cholesterol 220 mg

Sodium 580 mg

Excellent Source of Copper, Fiber, Iron, Magnesium, Manganese, Niacin, Phosphorus, Protein, Selenium, Thiamin, Vitamin B6, Vitamin B12, Vitamin C, Vitamin D, Vitamin K, Zinc.

Good Source of Calcium, Folate, Pantothenic Acid, Potassium, Vitamin A.

SPRING PASTA

Brilliantly colored garden vegetables and herbs tossed with linguini and covered in a light creamy sauce-this dish is freshness by the forkful.

- ¾ pound whole-wheat linguine
- 1 tablespoon olive oil
- 3 cloves garlic, minced
- 1 red bell pepper, seeded and cut into strips
- ½ pound thin asparagus, trimmed and cut into 2-inch pieces
- 1 cup grape or cherry tomatoes, sliced in half
- cup sliced button mushrooms
- 1 tablespoon all-purpose flour
- 1 cup low-sodium chicken broth
- ½ cup low-fat (1 %) milk
- ½ teaspoon salt
- ½ teaspoon freshly ground black pepper
- 1 large carrot, peeled and sliced into strips with a peeler (about 2 cups carrot ribbons)
- ½ cup (1 ½ ounces) grated Parmesan cheese
- ½ cup shredded basil

Bring a large pot of water to a boil. Add the pasta and cook until al dente according to the directions on the package. Before draining, reserve ½ cup of the pasta cooking water.

Heat the oil in a large skillet over medium-high heat. Cook the garlic, stirring, until softened, about 1 minute. Add the bell peppers and cook, stirring, until they begin to soften, about 3 minutes. Add the asparagus, tomatoes, and mushrooms. Cook, stirring, until softened, an additional 5 minutes. Stir in the flour and cook for 1 minute more.

Add the chicken broth, milk, salt, and pepper and bring to a boil ; reduce the heat to a simmer and cook until the liquid has thickened slightly, about 5 minutes. Stir in the carrot strips.

Toss the pasta with the vegetables and sauce, adding the pasta water, if necessary, to loosen the mixture. Serve garnished with the Parmesan and basil.

Makes 4 servings

Serving Size

2 cups pasta plus 2 tablespoon cheese and 1 tablespoon basil

Per Serving

Calories 490

Total Fat 11 g

Sat Fat 3 g Mono Fat 3 g Poly Fat 0.5 g

Protein 23 g

Carb 76 g

Fiber 10 g

Cholesterol 10 mg

Sodium 610 mg

Excellent Source of Calcium, Fiber, Potassium, Protein, Vitamin A, Vitamin C, Vitamin K

Good Source of Iron, Manganese, Niacin, Phosphorus, Riboflavin, Selenium, Vitamin B6

ASIAN NOODLE MIX

You can substitute whatever vegetables you have on hand to create this fabulous chicken, veggie, and noodle dish that is heady with Asian flavor and aroma.

- 8 ounces soba noodles or whole-wheat spaghetti
- 2 teaspoons canola oil
- 1 bunch scallions (white and green parts), sliced (¼ cup reserved for garnish)
- 1 tablespoon minced peeled fresh ginger
- 1 pound skinless boneless chicken breasts, thinly sliced
- 1 (15-ounce) can baby corn, drained
- ½ pound broccoli florets (about 3 cups)
- ½ pound fresh shiitake mushrooms, stemmed and sliced
- 1 red bell pepper, seeded and thinly sliced
- 1/3 cup low-sodium chicken broth
- ¼ cup low-sodium soy sauce

- 1 teaspoon toasted sesame oil

Bring a large pot of water to a boil. Add the noodles or pasta and cook according to the directions on the package.

Heat the canola oil in a wok or very large skillet over medium heat. Add the scallions and ginger and cook, stirring, until fragrant but not browned, about 30 seconds. Add the chicken and cook, stirring occasionally, until just cooked through, 4 to 5 minutes. Add the baby corn, broccoli, mushrooms, pepper slices, broth, and soy sauce and cook, stirring occasionally, until the broccoli is bright green and crisp-tender and the peppers are crisp-tender, 5 to 6 minutes. Add the noodles and sesame oil and toss to combine. Divide among 4 bowls and garnish with the reserved ¼ cup of scallions.

Makes 4 servings

Serving Size

2 ½ cups noodle mixture

Per Serving

Calories 540

Total Fat 8 g

Sat Fat 1 g Mono Fat 3.5 g Poly Fat 2.5 g

Protein 39 g

Carb 77 g

Fiber 11 g

Cholesterol 65 mg

Sodium 800 mg

Excellent Source of Fiber, Folate, Iron, Niacin, Phosphorus, Potassium, Protein, Riboflavin, Selenium, Vitamin A, Vitamin B6, Vitamin C, Vitamin K.

Good Source of Copper, Magnesium, Manganese, Pantothenic Acid, Thiamin, Zinc.

SHRIMP FRA DIAVOLO A LA POPEYE

This recipe is your cheat sheet for whipping up an incredible meal even when your fridge is empty, a tasty accomplishment you're sure to earn extra credit for with your family and friends. Just make sure you keep shrimp in the freezer-it thaws in five minutes-and although I call for fresh, you can substitute 1 ½ cups of frozen chopped spinach.

- ¾ pound whole-wheat thin spaghetti
- 2 tablespoons olive oil
- 1 medium red onion, thinly sliced
- 5 cloves garlic, minced
- 1 (14.5-ounce) can no-salt-added diced tomatoes
- 1 cup dry white wine
- 1 tablespoon tomato paste
- 1 teaspoon dried oregano
- ½ teaspoon crushed red pepper flakes
- ½ teaspoon salt
- ½ teaspoon freshly ground black pepper
- 1 pound large shrimp, peeled and deveined
- 3 cups lightly packed baby spinach leaves (3 ounces), coarsely chopped

Bring a large pot of water to a boil. Add the spaghetti and cook until al dente and according to the directions on the package.

While the pasta is cooking, heat 1 tablespoon of the oil in a large pot over medium-high heat. Add the onion and cook, stirring, until softened, about 3 minutes. Add the garlic and cook, stirring, for 1 additional minute. Add the tomatoes, wine, tomato paste, the remaining 1 tablespoon of olive oil, the oregano, red pepper flakes, salt, and pepper, and simmer until the sauce thickens slightly, 8 to 10 minutes. Add the shrimp and spinach and cook, stirring, until the shrimp is just cooked through, about 5 minutes. Remove from the heat. Add the drained cooked pasta to the sauce and toss until well combined.

Makes 4 servings

Serving Size

2 cups

Per Serving

Calories 580

Total Fat 10 g

Sat Fat 1.5 g Mono Fat 5.5 g Poly Fat 2 g

Protein 39 g

Carb 76 g

Fiber 13 g

Cholesterol 170 mg

Sodium 560 mg

Excellent Source of Copper, Fiber, Folate, Iron, Magnesium, Manganese, Niacin, Phosphorus, Protein, Selenium, Thiamin, Vitamin A, Vitamin B6, Vitamin B12, Vitamin C, Vitamin D, Vitamin K, Zinc.

Good Source of Pantothenic Acid, Potassium, Riboflavin.

MINT PENNE WITH ZUCCHINI

The bright, clean flavors and simplicity of this dish make it destined for regular rotation at your home as it is in mine. Toasting the garlic in the oil first infuses the dish with deep flavor and the fresh mint adds an unexpected wow factor.

- ¾ box (12 ounces) whole-wheat penne pasta
- ¼ cup olive oil
- 4 large cloves garlic, thinly sliced
- 2 medium zucchini (8 ounces each), sliced into ¼-inch-thick half moons
- 2 tablespoons fresh lemon juice
- 1 teaspoon finely grated lemon zest
- ¾ teaspoon salt
- ½ teaspoon freshly ground black pepper
- ½ cup freshly grated Parmesan cheese (1 ½ ounces)
- ¼ cup chopped fresh mint leaves

Bring a large pot of water to a boil. Add the penne and cook until al dente and according to the directions on the package.

Meanwhile, add the oil and garlic to a large deep skillet and cook over a medium-low heat, stirring frequently, until the garlic is lightly golden, about 6 minutes; be careful not to let the garlic burn. Add the zucchini. Cover and cook, stirring occasionally, until the zucchini is tender, 6 to 8 minutes. Remove from the heat. Stir in the lemon juice, zest, salt, and pepper.

Drain the pasta, then return it to the pasta pot. Add the zucchini mixture, Parmesan cheese, and mint, and toss to combine.

Makes 4 servings

Serving Size

2 cups

Per Serving

Calories 540

Total Fat 21 g

Sat Fat 4 g Mono Fat 10 g Poly Fat 2 g

Protein 19 g

Carb 71 g

Fiber 9 g

Cholesterol 10 mg

Sodium 710 mg

Excellent Source of Calcium, Fiber, Protein, Vitamin C.

Good Source of Iron, Manganese, Potassium, Vitamin B6.

PASTA WITH CRAB AND ASPARAGUS

Succulent crab mingled with fresh, fragrant herbs and crisp tender asparagus in a wine-infused lemon garlic sauce. It's a simple pasta dish, effortlessly elevated to fabulous.

- 12 ounces whole-wheat fettuccine
- 2 tablespoons olive oil
- 4 cloves garlic, thinly sliced
- 1 cup dry white wine
- 1 cup fish stock or water
- 1 bunch (¾ pound) asparagus, trimmed and cut into 1-inch pieces
- 3 tablespoons fresh lemon juice
- 2 teaspoons finely grated lemon zest
- ½ teaspoon salt
- ¼ teaspoon freshly ground black pepper
- 1 pound cooked lump crabmeat, drained
- ¼ cup chopped fresh parsley, plus more for garnish
- ¼ cup chopped fresh tarragon, plus more for garnish

Bring a large pot of water to a boil. Add the fettuccine and cook until al dente and according to the directions on the package.

Meanwhile, add the oil and garlic to a large deep skillet and cook over low heat, stirring, until the garlic is lightly golden, about 5 minutes; be careful not to let the garlic burn. Add the wine and stock and bring to a boil; reduce the heat to a vigorous simmer and cook until the liquid has reduced slightly, about 5 minutes. Add the asparagus, lemon juice, lemon zest, salt, and pepper and cook until the asparagus is just cooked, about 3 minutes. Add the crabmeat and ¼ cup each of parsley and tarragon, and stir to combine until the crabmeat is heated through, 1 to 2 minutes.

Drain the pasta and return it to the pasta pot. Add the crabmeat mixture and stir to combine. Serve garnished with the additional herbs.

Makes 4 servings

Serving Size

3 cups pasta mixture, ¼ cup sauce, and 1 tablespoon each parsley and tarragon garnish

Per Serving

Calories 570

Total Fat 11 g

Sat Fat 1.5 g Mono Fat 5.5 g Poly Fat 2.5 g

Protein 40 g

Carb 73 g

Fiber 13 g

Cholesterol 115 mg

Sodium 820 mg

Excellent Source of Calcium, Copper, Fiber, Folate, Iron, Magnesium, Manganese, Niacin, Phosphorus, Potassium, Protein, Selenium, Thiamin, Vitamin A, Vitamin B6, Vitamin B12, Vitamin C, Vitamin K, Zinc.

Good Source of Pantothenic Acid, Riboflavin.

SIMPLE RAVIOLI TOSS

This recipe barely counts as cooking, yet you can take full credit as everyone devours it. It is one of those "saves the day" dishes you will make over and over again.

- 4 plum tomatoes (about ¾ pound), chopped (about 2 cups)
- 1 (12-ounce) jar roasted red peppers, drained, rinsed, and chopped
- 2 tablespoons olive oil
- 1 ½ tablespoons red wine vinegar
- 1 clove garlic, minced
- Salt and freshly ground black pepper to taste
- 1 pound store-bought fresh or frozen cheese ravioli, preferably whole-wheat
- 5 cups arugula leaves, coarsely chopped (about 5 ounces)

In a large bowl, combine the tomatoes, roasted peppers, olive oil, vinegar, and garlic. Season to taste with salt and black pepper. Let the vegetable mixture sit at room temperature while you are cooking the ravioli.

Cook the ravioli according the directions on the package. Drain and add to the vegetables along with the arugula. Toss and serve at once.

Makes 4 servings

Serving Size

2 cups

Per Serving

Calories 460

Total Fat 20 g

Sat Fat 8 g Mono Fat 5 g Poly Fat 1. 5 g

Protein 19 g

Carb 52 g

Fiber 7 g

Cholesterol 75 mg

Sodium 1000 mg

Excellent Source of Calcium, Fiber, Protein, Vitamin A, Vitamin C, Vitamin K.

Good Source of Iron.

Eating Well Tip

Yes, you can have that big bowlful of pasta you crave without overdoing carbs or calories. The secret is keeping servings to a generous, but not excessive, 3 ounces of uncooked pasta per person (1 ½ cups cooked), and amping it up with lots of vegetables and chunks of lean protein. Also, go for whole-wheat pasta, which is no longer the cardboard of yore. Now they make it tender and mild and even have whole-wheat blends for the best of both worlds.

DINNER-KICKIN' BACK

These meals are supremely satisfying- soups, stews, chili, marinated meats, roasted vegetables, steak house-inspired dinners, and comfort casseroles that will feed a crowd. Each is designed so you can Put extraordinary food on the table without putting akinkinthatlaid-backfeeling.

ENTRECOTE STEAK WITH MUSTARD SAUCE AND PARMESAN STEAK "FRIES"

This flavor-packed sauce is a breeze to whip up and brings out the most in the juicy beef. Served with ripe beefsteak tomato slices and steak "fries," this meal really satisfies that steak house craving.

- 4 teaspoons canola oil
- 1 small shallot, finely chopped (about ¼ cup)
- 1 tablespoon all-purpose flour
- 2 cups low-sodium chicken broth
- 1 boneless sirloin steak, about 1 ¼ pounds
- ¼ teaspoon salt, plus more to taste
- 1/8 teaspoon freshly ground black pepper, plus more to taste
- 3 tablespoons whole-grain mustard
- 2 large ripe beefsteak tomatoes, thickly sliced

In a medium saucepan, heat 2 teaspoons of the oil over medium heat. Add the shallot and cook, stirring, until softened, about 2 minutes. Stir in the flour and cook for 30 seconds. Stir in the broth, bring to a boil, and cook until reduced to 1 cup, about 10 minutes.

Meanwhile, cook the steak. Pat the steak dry and sprinkle both sides with ¼ teaspoon of salt and 1/8 teaspoon of pepper. Heat the remaining 2 teaspoons of oil in a heavy skillet over medium-high heat. Cook the steak, turning once, for 6 to 8 minutes total for medium rare, or to desired doneness. Transfer to a cutting board and cover with foil to keep warm.

Discard the fat from the pan. Add the reduced stock mixture and bring to a simmer, being sure to scrape up any brown bits from the bottom of the pan. Stir in the mustard and season to taste with salt and pepper. Pour any juices that have accumulated on the board into the sauce.

Thinly slice the steak and divide among 4 plates. Spoon the sauce over the steak and serve the sliced tomatoes and the "fries" alongside.

Makes 4 servings

Serving Size

5 to 7 slices steak, about 2 tablespoons sauce, 3 tomato slices, and 4 wedges of "fries "

Per Serving

Calories 430

Total Fat

15 g Sat Fat 3 g Mono Fat 7 g Poly Fat 3 g

Protein 32 g

Carb 42 g

Fiber 3 g

Cholesterol 40 mg

Sodium 640 mg

Excellent Source of Iron, Manganese, Niacin, Phosphorus, Potassium, Protein, Selenium, Vitamin B6, Vitamin C, Vitamin K, Zinc.

Good Source of Calcium, Copper, Fiber, Folate, Magnesium, Pantothenic Acid, Riboflavin, Thiamin, Vitamin A, Vitamin B12.

Eating Well Tip

Thinly slicing steak is a great way to make an appropriate serving look more plentiful and be more satisfying.

PARMESAN STEAK " FRIES "

If you know anything about me, you know that French fries are my weakness. I love them every which way-thick, thin, fast-food, or fancy restaurant style. I've been on a mission to get my fry fix in a healthier way. With these thick, tender-on-the-inside, crisp-on-the- outside, Parmesan-crusted wedges I am happy to say: mission accomplished.

- Cooking spray
- 3 large russet potatoes (about 1 ½ pounds total), unpeeled
- 1 ½ tablespoon canola oil
- ¼ cup grated Parmesan cheese (¾ ounce)
- Salt to taste

Preheat the oven to 450°F. Spray a baking sheet with cooking spray.

Cut each of the potatoes in half lengthwise. Rest each half on its flat side and cut each half lengthwise, straight down into 4 even slices. You will have 16 slices altogether. Cut the rounded edge off of the outermost slices so each slice can lie completely flat on either side. Put the potatoes into a medium-size bowl and toss with the oil.

Place the potatoes on the prepared baking sheet and bake for 20 minutes. Sprinkle the potatoes with cheese and continue to bake for another 15 to 20 minutes, until they are crisp and golden brown; there is no need to turn them. Season with salt and serve immediately.

Makes 4 servings

Serving Size

4 wedges

PORCINI CRUSTED FILET MIGNON WITH HERBED POTATOES AND CREAMED SPINACH

A crust of ground porcini mushrooms that crisps as the steak cooks gives the tender meat an incredible flavor and texture you can't quite put your finger on if you are not in the know. It's a huge reward for a little extra effort. Served with the mashed potatoes and creamed spinach, it is the centerpiece of the ultimate inspired comfort food dinner.

- 1/3 cup (1/3 ounce) dried porcini mushrooms
- 4 (1-inch-thick) filet mignon steaks (about 1 ¼ pounds total)
- ¼ teaspoon salt
- 1/8 teaspoon freshly ground black pepper
- Cooking spray

Process the dried porcini mushrooms in a spice mill or the small bowl of a food processor until they are a fine powder; it's okay if the powder isn't uniform and there are some larger pieces. Transfer the ground mushrooms to a plate. Season the steaks with the salt and pepper on both sides, then press the steaks into the mushroom powder until well coated on both sides.

Spray a large nonstick skillet with cooking spray and preheat over medium heat. Cook the steaks for about 6 minutes per side for medium rare, or to desired doneness. Serve with the Herbed Mashed Potatoes and Creamed Spinach.

Makes 4 servings

Serving Size

1 steak, ¾ cup mashed potatoes, and ¾ cup creamed spinach

Per Serving

Calories 460

Total Fat 14 g

Sat Fat 6 g Mono Fat 5 g Poly Fat 1 g

Protein 42 g

Carb 46 g

Fiber 8 g

Cholesterol 95 mg

Sodium 550 mg

Excellent Source of Calcium, Fiber, Folate, Iodine, Iron, Magnesium, Manganese, Niacin, Phosphorus, Potassium, Protein, Riboflavin, Selenium, Thiamin, Vitamin A, Vitamin B6, Vitamin Bl2 ,Vitamin C, Vitamin K, Zinc

Good Source of Copper, Pantothenic Acid, Vitamin D.

HERBED MASHED POTATOES

The heady herbal aroma tells you half the story of how good these potatoes are before you even try them. The pool of melted butter tells you more. Then the picture is complete with the first creamy, luxurious bite. Feel free to use whatever herb combination you have around the house; just about any tender herb-parsley, chervil, or dill-works here.

- 1 ¼ pounds Yukon Gold potatoes (about 4 medium) , peeled and cut into l-inch pieces
- ½ cup low-fat (1%) milk
- 2 ½ teaspoons finely chopped fresh chives
- 2 teaspoons finely chopped fresh tarragon leaves
- ¼ teaspoon salt, plus more to taste
- 4 ½ teaspoons butter

Place the potatoes in a steamer basket fitted over a large pot of boiling water. Cover and steam until the potatoes are knife-tender, 12 to 15 minutes. Meanwhile, heat the milk in a saucepan over low heat until hot. When the potatoes are done, drain the water and transfer the potatoes to the pot. Add the hot milk and mash to the desired consistency. Stir in the chives, tarragon, and salt. Serve with a teaspoon of butter on top of each serving.

Makes 4 servings

Serving Size

¾ cup

CREAMED SPINACH WITH SHALLOTS AND NUTMEG POWDER

I love creamed spinach so much I decided to make it easy enough and healthy enough to enjoy every day. The easy factor comes from using frozen spinach, which is not noticeably different from fresh-cooked in this dish, and the healthy factor comes from a revamped cream sauce made with thickened low-fat milk. A finishing touch of all-natural evaporated milk gives another hit of creaminess without the downsides. If you are skeptical, try it. I have won over the most ardent purists.

- 2 (10-ounce) packages frozen chopped spinach, thawed
- 2 teaspoons olive oil
- 2 small shallots, finely chopped (about ½ cup)
- 4 teaspoons all-purpose flour
- 1½ cups low-fat (1%) milk
- ½ cup low-sodium chicken broth
- 2 tablespoons evaporated milk
- Pinch of ground nutmeg
- Salt and freshly ground black pepper to taste

Squeeze all of the water from the spinach. In a large saucepan, heat the oil over medium heat. Add the shallots and cook, stirring, until softened, about 2 minutes. Add the flour to the pan and cook, stirring, for 30 seconds. Add the low-fat milk and broth and cook, scraping up any bits from the bottom of the pan. Bring to a simmer and cook for 2 minutes. Add the spinach and simmer until tender, about 5 minutes. Stir in the evaporated milk and nutmeg, and season to taste with salt and pepper.

Makes 4 servings

Serving Size

¾ cup

Eating Well Tip

Evaporated milk is one of my secret weapons in the quest for creamy. It is pure, real milk that has had most of its water evaporated off so it's extra thick and rich. In many recipes it is a great stand-in for cream but with half the calories and a quarter of the fat.

HERBED BEEF STEW WITH BUTTERNUT SQUASH

Far from your run-of-the-mill beef stew, this one transports you to another land with a unique combination of everyday ingredients. In it tender beef is nestled with chunks of sweet butternut squash in a rich Moroccan spiced tomato sauce. That exotic inspiration continues as it is served over fluffy couscous and topped with crunchy almonds. It's just as easy as, if not easier than, the same-old stew, but so much more rewarding.

- 2 teaspoons olive oil
- 1 pound stew beef (round or chuck), cut into chunks
- 1 large onion, chopped
- 1 tablespoon minced peeled fresh ginger
- 2 cloves garlic, minced
- 1 pound peeled cubed butternut squash, cut into 1 ½-inch cubes (about 2 ½ cups)
- (14.5-ounce) can no-salt-added diced tomatoes
- 1 (8-ounce) can no-salt-added tomato sauce
- 1 ½ cups low-sodium beef broth
- 1 ½ teaspoons ground cumin
- 1 teaspoon ground cinnamon
- ½ teaspoon crushed red pepper flakes
- cups cooked whole-wheat couscous
- ¼ cup sliced almonds, toasted in a dry skillet over medium-high heat, stirring frequently, until golden brown and fragrant, about 2 minutes
- teaspoons minced fresh parsley
- 2 ½ teaspoons finely chopped fresh chives
- 2 teaspoons finely chopped fresh tarragon leaves

Heat the oil in a 4-quart saucepan over medium-high heat. Add the beef and cook until browned on all sides, about 5 minutes. Transfer the meat to a plate, leaving the juices in the saucepan. Add the onion and cook, stirring, until softened and translucent, about 6 minutes.

Add the ginger and garlic and cook, stirring, for 1 additional minute. Return the beef to the pot and stir in the squash, diced tomatoes, tomato sauce, beef broth, cumin, cinnamon, and red pepper flakes.

Bring to a boil, then reduce the heat to a simmer. Add the tarragon. Cover and cook until the beef is tender, 30 to 35 minutes.

Spoon the stew over the couscous, and sprinkle each serving with almonds, parsley, chives.

Makes 4 servings

Serving Size

1 ¾ cups stew, ¾ cups couscous, and 1 tablespoon almonds

Per Serving

Calories 490

Total Fat 13 g

Sat Fat 3 g Mono Fat 6 g Poly Fat 2 g

Protein 35 g

Carb 57 g

Fiber 8 g

Cholesterol 65 mg

Sodium 150 mg

Excellent Source of Copper, Fiber, Iron, Magnesium, Manganese, Niacin, Phosphorus, Potassium, Protein, Riboflavin, Selenium, Thiamin, Vitamin A, Vitamin B6, Vitamin B12, Vitamin C, Vitamin K, Zinc.

Good Source of Calcium, Folate, Pantothenic Acid.

AROMATIC STEAK WITH CHEESE SAUCE

This recipe is a collision of intense umami flavors-steak, balsamic vinegar, aged cheese, grilled onion, and a spike of Worcestershire. Eaten together over peppery radicchio with a side of Grilled Garlic Bread, they make a big bang of deliciousness.

- 3 tablespoons olive oil
- 1 tablespoon balsamic vinegar
- 1 teaspoon brown sugar
- 2 cloves garlic, minced
- 1 ½ pounds flank steak Cooking spray
- 1 medium red onion, cut into ½-inch-thick rounds
- ½ teaspoon salt
- ¼ teaspoon freshly ground black pepper
- 3 tablespoons crumbled blue cheese
- 3 tablespoons low-fat buttermilk
- Dash of Worcestershire sauce
- 12 radicchio leaves
- 2 tablespoon chopped fresh parsley

In a small bowl, whisk together 2 tablespoons of the olive oil, the balsamic vinegar, brown sugar, and garlic. Put the steak into a sealable plastic bag with the marinade and put in the refrigerator for at least 1 hour and up to 8 hours. Allow the meat to come to room temperature before cooking.

Spray a large grill pan with cooking spray and preheat it over

medium-high heat, or prepare an outdoor grill. Brush both sides of the onion slices with the remaining tablespoon of oil and grill until they are softened, about 6 minutes per side. Separate into rings and set aside.

Remove the meat from the marinade and season both sides with salt and pepper. Discard the marinade. Grill the meat over medium-high heat for about 5 minutes per side for medium rare. Let rest for 5 to 10 minutes before slicing thinly on a bias.

In a small bowl, combine the blue cheese and buttermilk with a fork, mashing until creamy. Stir in the Worcestershire sauce.

Arrange 3 radicchio leaves and a pile of onions on each serving plate. Top with the slices of steak. Drizzle with the blue cheese sauce and top with a sprinkle of parsley.

Makes 4 servings

Serving Size

5 to 7 slices steak, 1 ½ tablespoons blue cheese sauce, about 6 onion rings

Per Serving

Calories 330

Total Fat 18 g

Sat Fat 5 g Mono Fat 9 g Poly Fat 1.5 g

Protein 34 g

Carb 7 g

Fiber 1 g

Cholesterol 50 mg

Sodium 480 mg

Excellent Source of Niacin, Phosphorus, Protein, Selenium, Vitamin B6, Vitamin B12, Vitamin K, Zinc.

Good Source of Copper, Folate, Iron, Magnesium, Pantothenic Acid, Potassium, Riboflavin, Vitamin C.

BAKED BEANS WITH HAM AND CITRUS CABBAGE SALAD

These tangy sweet baked beans have big chunks of smoky ham-and lots of them-making it a main course that even satisfies the likes of my devotedly carnivorous husband.

- 2 teaspoons canola oil
- 1 medium onion, diced
- 12 ounces smoked Virginia ham, cut into ¼ -inch cubes
- 2 cloves garlic, minced
- 2 (15-ounce) cans navy beans (preferably low-sodium) , drained and rinsed
- 1 (I 5-ounce) can crushed tomatoes (preferably no salt added)
- ½ cup water
- ¼ cup unsulfured molasses
- 1 tablespoon Dijon mustard
- 1 tablespoon cider vinegar
- ½ teaspoon freshly ground black pepper

Heat the oil in a large skillet over medium-high heat. Add the onion and cook until softened and translucent, about 5 minutes. Add the ham and garlic and cook for an additional 3 minutes. Stir in the beans, crushed tomatoes, water, molasses, mustard, vinegar, and pepper.

Bring to a boil, then reduce the heat to a simmer. Cover and cook until about half of the liquid is absorbed, 15 minutes. Serve alongside the Green Apple and Cabbage Salad.

Makes 4 servings

Serving Size

1 ¼ cups baked beans and 1 ¾ cups salad

Per Serving

Calories 570

Total Fat 13 g

Sat Fat 2 g Mono Fat 6.5 g Poly Fat 2.5 g

Protein 33 g

Carb 81 g

Fiber 18 g

Cholesterol 45 mg

Sodium 1260 mg

Excellent Source of Calcium, Fiber, Iron, Magnesium, Manganese, Niacin, Phosphorus, Potassium, Protein, Selenium, Thiamin, Vitamin A, Vitamin B6, Vitamin C, Vitamin K, Zinc.

Good Source of Copper, Iodine, Riboflavin.

CITRUS CABBAGE SALAD

This crisp bright salad is like a rough-cut, chunky slaw with a tangy vinaigrette dressing. It is refreshing and hearty all at once.

- 5 tablespoons red wine vinegar
- ¼ cup water
- 2 tablespoons sugar
- 4 teaspoons canola oil
- 1 ½ teaspoons Dijon mustard
- ½ teaspoon salt
- ¼ teaspoon freshly ground black pepper
- 1 small head red cabbage (1 pound), leaves cut into 1-inch squares
- 1 large green apple (about 8 ounces), skin on, cored and sliced into thin half-moons
- 3 scallions (white and green parts), chopped (about ½ cup)

In a large bowl, whisk together the vinegar, water, sugar, oil, mustard, salt, and pepper. Add the cabbage, apple, and scallions and toss to combine.

Makes 4 servings

Serving Size

1 ¾ cups salad

HAM-WRAPPED ENDIVE TART AND GREEN SALAD WITH SHALLOT VINAIGRETTE

I first had this gratin at a neighbor's Belgian food and beer tasting, which was part of a fund-raiser for our children's school. Days later I couldn't get this rich cheesy bake out of my mind. I've lightened it without losing the sumptuous flavor by making the sauce with low-fat milk and holding the butter, and I made it easier by "blanching" the endive in the same pan as you bake it in. It is just as heavenly as I remember it.

- 8 small heads Belgian endive (about 1 ½ pounds)
- 8 medium-thick slices Black Forest ham (about ½ pound)
- 1 ½ cups cold low-fat (1 %) milk
- 3 tablespoons all-purpose flour
- Pinch of ground nutmeg
- ¼ teaspoon salt
- ¼ teaspoon freshly ground black pepper
- ½ cup packed grated Gruyere cheese (3 ounces)
- 4 thick slices crusty dark brown bread

1 recipe Green Salad with Shallot Preheat the oven to 350°F.

Cut the bottom off of each endive, removing just enough so they remain intact. Rinse clean and, without drying, place in a 9 x1 3-inch microwave-safe baking dish. Cover tightly with plastic wrap and microwave for 8 minutes. Transfer the endive to paper towels until cool enough to handle, about 5 minutes. Wipe out the baking dish. Wrap each endive with a slice of ham and place in the baking dish.

In a medium saucepan, whisk together the cold milk and flour until the flour is dissolved. Heat over high heat, whisking constantly, until the mixture thickens and comes to a boil, about 5 minutes. Remove from the heat. Add the nutmeg, salt, and pepper. Spoon the sauce over the endive rolls, spreading it out evenly. Sprinkle with the cheese and bake until bubbling and golden brown, 30 to 40 minutes. Serve with the bread and Green Salad with Shallot Dressing.

Makes 4 servings

Serving Size

2 pieces endive, 1 thick slice bread, and 2 cups salad

Per Serving

Calories 420

Total Fat 18 g

Sat Fat 6 g Mono Fat 8 g Poly Fat 2 g

Protein 27 g

Carb 39 g

Fiber 9 g

Cholesterol 60 mg

Sodium 1070 mg

Excellent Source of Calcium, Fiber, Folate, Manganese, Phosphorus, Protein, Riboflavin, Selenium, Thiamin, Vitamin A, Vitamin C.

Good Source of Copper, Iodine, Iron, Magnesium, Niacin, Pantothenic Acid, Potassium, Vitamin B6, Vitamin B12, Vitamin D, Zinc.

PAELLA WITH CHORIZO AND GREEN OLIVES

This luscious dish of moist golden rice studded with juicy chicken, smoky sausage, and mouthwatering olives is a heartwarming meal that has both down-home and upscale appeal. It is deceptively easy to make and it reheats well, in case you're lucky enough to have leftovers.

- 1 tablespoon plus 2 teaspoons olive oil
- 3 ounces chorizo sausage, casing removed, sliced into ¼-inch rounds
- 1 pound skinless boneless chicken thighs, cut into 1-inch pieces
- 1 medium onion, chopped
- 2 cloves garlic, minced
- 2 ½ cups low-sodium chicken broth
- 1 (10-ounce) package frozen peas
- 1 cup uncooked white rice
- 1 large ripe tomato, chopped
- ¼ cup sliced green Spanish pimento-stuffed olives
- ½ teaspoon salt
- ¼ teaspoon freshly ground black pepper
- 1/8 teaspoon ground turmeric
- Small pinch of saffron threads

Preheat the oven to 375°F. Heat 1 tablespoon of the oil in a large, heavy skillet over medium-high heat (use a skillet that has a cover). Add the chorizo and cook, stirring occasionally, until browned, about 3 minutes. Add the chicken and cook, stirring occasionally, until browned, about 5 minutes. Transfer the chicken and chorizo to a plate.

Heat the remaining 2 teaspoons of oil in the skillet. Add the onions and cook, stirring, until softened and translucent, 3 to 5 minutes. Add the garlic and cook, stirring, for 1 additional minute. Return the chicken and chorizo to the skillet and add the chicken broth, peas, rice, tomato, olives, salt, pepper, turmeric, and saffron. Bring to a boil, cover, and transfer to oven. Cook until the rice is tender and the liquid is absorbed, 25 to 30 minutes.

Makes 4 servings

Serving Size

2 cups

Per Serving

Calories 610

Total Fat 25 g

Sat Fat 7 g Mono Fat 12 .5 g Poly Fat 4.5 g

Protein 37 g

Carb 55 g

Fiber 5 g

Cholesterol 95 mg

Sodium 910 mg

Excellent Source of Folate, Iron, Manganese, Niacin, Phosphorus, Potassium, Protein, Riboflavin, Selenium, Thiamin, Vitamin A, Vitamin B6, Vitamin C, Vitamin K, Zinc .

Good Source of Copper, Fiber, Magnesium, Pantothenic Acid, Vitamin B12.

CHICKEN AND GRAPE SKEWERS WITH LENTILS

Juicy green grapes give these chicken skewers a big wow factor. The fruit softens, sweetens, and plumps further on the grill, providing an unexpected counterpoint to the savory, citrus-laced poultry.

- 2 tablespoons olive oil
- 1 tablespoon fresh lemon juice
- ½ teaspoon finely grated lemon zest
- 2 cloves garlic, minced
- 1 teaspoon ground cumin
- ½ teaspoon ground coriander
- ½ teaspoon salt
- 1 pound skinless boneless chicken breasts, cut into ¾-inch cubes
- 8 (10-inch) skewers
- 1 ½ cups seedless green grapes
- Cooking spray
- 2 tablespoons chopped fresh mint leaves
- lemon, cut into wedges

In a medium-size bowl, whisk together the oil, lemon juice, zest, garlic, cumin, coriander, and salt. Add the chicken to the marinade and toss to coat. Marinate the chicken in the refrigerator for at least 20 minutes and up to 4 hours. While the chicken is marinating, soak the skewers in water if wooden.

Thread the chicken cubes onto the skewers, alternating them with grapes. Spray a grill pan with cooking spray and preheat over medium-high heat, or prepare an outdoor grill. Grill the chicken until cooked through, 3 to 4 minutes per side. Sprinkle with the mint and serve with the pilaf and lemon wedges.

Makes 4 servings

Serving Size

2 skewers (each skewer has 4 pieces of chicken and 4 grapes) and ¾ cup pilaf

Per Serving

Calories 450

Total Fat 16 g

Sat Fat 2.5 g Mono Fat 9 g Poly Fat 2 g

Protein 36 g

Carb 45 g

Fiber 10 g

Cholesterol 65 mg

Sodium 680 mg

Excellent Source of Fiber, Iron, Niacin, Phosphorus, Potassium, Protein, Selenium, Vitamin A, Vitamin B6, Vitamin C, Vitamin K.

Good Source of Manganese, Thiamin.

LENTILS PILAF

This delightful dish is like a warm salad brimming with garden fresh flavor, color, and aroma. It is delicious and satisfying on its own as a light meal or vegetarian entree, but it is a wonderful accompaniment to the chicken and grape skewers. It is important to use green or French lentils here because, unlike other varieties, they hold their shape when cooked.

- 1 cup green lentils
- 2 cups water
- 2 tablespoons olive oil
- 2 tablespoons diced shallots
- 3 cups baby spinach leaves (about 3 ounces)
- 1 cup halved grape tomatoes (about ½ pint)
- ¼ cup chopped fresh basil leaves
- ¼ cup chopped fresh mint leaves
- ¼ cup chopped fresh parsley
- 2 tablespoons fresh lemon juice
- ¼ teaspoon salt
- ¼ teaspoon freshly ground black pepper

Place the lentils in a pot with the water and bring to a boil. Reduce the heat, cover, and simmer until the lentils are tender but still retain their shape, 30 to 35 minutes. Drain any excess water from the lentils and set them aside.

Heat the olive oil in a large skillet over medium-high heat. Add the shallots and cook, stirring, until softened, about 3 minutes. Add the spinach and cook untiljust wilted, about 2 minutes. Add the tomatoes, cooked lentils, basil, mint, and parsley to the pan and stir to combine. Cook until warmed through, about 1 minute. Stir in the lemon juice, salt, and pepper, and serve.

Makes 4 servings

Serving Size

¾ cup

AROMATIC TURKEY WITH ROASTED POTATOES AND BRUSSELS SPROUTS

Fresh roasted turkey breast isn't something you think of making regularly, but it should be! It couldn't be simpler to cook and it gives enough juicy lean meat to feed a crowd or have fabulous leftovers for sandwiches and other dishes the next few days. This lemon, garlic, and rosemary version with its quick pan sauce alongside crisp-tender roasted vegetables means you can have a Thanksgiving-worthy turkey dinner in less than 90 minutes any week of the year.

- 1 tablespoon olive oil
- 2 teaspoons finely chopped fresh rosemary
- 2 teaspoons finely grated lemon zest
- 1 teaspoon salt
- ½ teaspoon freshly ground black pepper
- 1 whole bone-in turkey breast, skin removed (about 6 pounds)
- 2 cups low-sodium chicken broth
- 4 small cloves garlic, peeled
- 3 tablespoons fresh lemon juice

Preheat the oven to 375°F.

In a small bowl, combine the oil, rosemary, lemon zest, ¾ teaspoon salt, and ¼ teaspoon pepper. Place the turkey in a medium-sized flame-proof roasting pan, breast side up, and rub the rosemary-lemon mixture onto the breast. Pour 1 cup of the broth into the dish and add the garlic and half of the lemon juice.

Roast, uncovered, until the juices run clear when pierced and a meat thermometer registers 165°F, 1 to 1 hours. Transfer the turkey breast to a carving board and allow it to rest for 10 minutes before carving.

Place the pan directly on top of the stove. Add the remaining 1 cup of broth and cook over high heat until it comes to a boil, scraping up any browned bits and allowing them to dissolve in the broth, and mashing the garlic cloves into the broth. Cook over high heat until the broth is reduced by roughly half, about 6 minutes. Stir in the remaining lemon juice and remaining VI teaspoon each of salt and pepper.

Carve the turkey and serve topped with the sauce. Serve alongside the mashed potatoes and Brussels sprouts.

Makes 8 servings

Serving Size

4 ¼-inch slices turkey, 2 tablespoons sauce, ¾ cup potatoes, and ¾ cup Brussels sprouts

Per Serving

Calories 600

Total Fat 11 g

Sat Fat 2 g Mono Fat 7 g Poly Fat 2 g

Protein 80 g

Carb 40 g

Fiber 7 g

Cholesterol 200 mg

Sodium 770 mg

Excellent Source of Copper, Fiber, Folate, Iron, Magnesium, Manganese, Niacin, Pantothenic Acid, Phosphorus, Potassium, Protein, Riboflavin, Selenium, Thiamin, Vitamin B6, Vitamin C, Vitamin K, Zinc.

Good Source of Vitamin A, Vitamin B12.

ROASTED POTATOES

Crunchy and golden brown outside with a tender soft center, these rosemary-spiked potatoes are absolutely heavenly. And you hardly have to do a thing.

- 2 ½ pounds small red new potatoes, halved
- 2 tablespoons olive oil
- 2 teaspoons chopped fresh rosemary leaves, or ¾ teaspoon dried
- ½ teaspoons salt

Preheat the oven to 375°F.

Place the potatoes on a baking sheet and toss them with the oil, rosemary, and salt. Roast until they are golden brown and crisp on the outside and softened and tender on the inside, about 1 ¼ hours.

Makes 8 servings

Serving Size

¾ cup

BRUSSELS SPROUTS

I have turned around countless Brussels sprout naysayers with this simple dish. In the oven the humble vegetable is transformed. Its outer leaves crisp and its natural sugars caramelize the outside, while the inside becomes yieldingly tender. Its flavor mellows to a delightfully nutty essence. I wish I could be there to see your face light up when you taste them.

- 2 pounds Brussels sprouts, halved
- 2 tablespoons olive oil
- ½ teaspoon salt

Preheat the oven to 375°F.

Place the Brussels sprouts on a baking sheet and toss them with the oil and salt. Roast until they are golden brown and crisp on the outside and softened and tender inside, about 1 hour.

Makes 8 servings

Serving Size

¾ cup

SIMPLE TURKEY CHILI

To me, chili is the ultimate one-pot meal. It's a breeze to make and satisfying to eat, and the variations are only limited by your imagination. This one is all white-with white beans, turkey, and white corn (hominy)-with hints of green from flavorful poblano peppers. Double the recipe and you have a party. Just put out the fixin's and let guests help themselves.

- 1 tablespoon canola oil
- 1 medium onion, diced
- 2 stalks celery, diced
- 3 medium poblano peppers, seeded, white ribs removed, and finely diced
- 1 clove garlic, minced
- 1 teaspoon ground cumin
- ½ teaspoon ground coriander
- ¼ teaspoon cayenne pepper, plus more to taste
- 1 pound ground white-meat turkey
- 2 (1 5.5-ounce) cans white beans (such as cannelini; preferably low sodium), drained and rinsed
- 4 cups low-sodium chicken broth
- ¾ teaspoon dried oregano
- 1 (15.5-ounce) can hominy, drained and rinsed
- ¾ teaspoon salt, plus more to taste
- ¼ cup reduced-fat sour cream
- 2 tablespoons chopped fresh cilantro
- Lime wedges

Heat the oil in a large pot or Dutch oven over medium heat. Add the onion, celery, and poblano peppers and cook, stirring occasionally, until the vegetables are softened, about 8 minutes. Add the garlic, cumin, coriander, and ¼ teaspoon of cayenne and cook, stirring, until fragrant, about 30 seconds.

Add the ground turkey and cook, breaking up the meat with a spoon, until the meat is no longer pink, about 2 minutes. Add the white beans, broth, and oregano. Cook, partially covered and stirring occasionally, for 25 minutes.

Add the hominy, ¾ teaspoon of salt, and more cayenne pepper to taste and continue cooking, partially covered, for 10 minutes longer. Ladle into individual bowls and top each serving with 1 tablespoon of sour cream and 1 ½ teaspoons of cilantro. Garnish with a lime wedge.

Makes 4 servings

Serving Size

21/4 cups, 1 tablespoon sour cream, and 1 ½ teaspoons cilantro

Per Serving

Calories 490

Total Fat 11 g

Sat Fat 2 g Mono Fat 3 g Poly Fat 2 g

Protein 47 g

Carb 55 g

Fiber 13 g

Cholesterol 55 mg

Sodium 900 mg

Excellent Source of Fiber, Iron, Magnesium, Phosphorus, Potassium, Protein, Riboflavin, Thiamin, Vitamin C, Vitamin K, Zinc.

Good Source of Calcium, Copper, Iodine, Manganese, Niacin, Vitamin A.

CLASSIC TUNA NOODLE CASSEROLE

Who doesn't have fond childhood memories of mom's tuna noodle casserole? This one brings you right back to that warm fuzzy place, but it tastes better than you remembered because it is better. With a simple from-scratch cream sauce and chunks of fresh mushrooms subbing for the condensed soup, plus lots of bright green vegetables and pasta that is tender but not mushy, it's a welcomed retro remake.

- ¾ pound whole-wheat fettuccine
- 1 tablespoon canola oil
- small onion, chopped
- 1 large stalk celery, finely diced
- 10 ounces white mushrooms, stemmed and chopped
- ¼ cup all-purpose flour
- cups low-fat (1 %) milk
- 1 cup low-sodium chicken broth or vegetable broth
- ¾ teaspoon salt
- ¼ teaspoon freshly ground black pepper
- (6-ounce) cans chunk light tuna in water, drained
- 1 (10-ounce) box frozen chopped broccoli, thawed
- 1 (10-ounce) box frozen peas, thawed
- 1/3 cup plain bread crumbs
- tablespoons freshly grated Parmesan cheese

Preheat the oven to 425°F.

Bring a large pot of water to a boil. Break the fettuccine into thirds, and cook until tender but firm, a minute or two less than the package directions call for. Drain.

Heat the oil in a large deep skillet over medium heat. Add the onion and cook, stirring, until softened, 5 minutes. Add the celery and cook, stirring occasionally, until just tender, 6 minutes. Add the mushrooms and cook until they release their water, about 5 minutes more.

Sprinkle the flour over the mushroom mixture and stir immediately to incorporate. Add the milk and broth and bring the mixture to a boil, stirring frequently. Reduce the heat to medium-low and cook, stirring occasionally, until the liquid has thickened, about 8 minutes. Add the salt and pepper, cooked fettuccine, tuna, broccoli, and peas, and toss to incorporate. Pour mixture into a 9x 13-inch casserole dish.

In a small bowl, combine the bread crumbs and Parmesan cheese. Sprinkle them over the casserole and bake until bubbly, about 25 minutes.

Makes 6 servings

Serving Size

2 ½ cups

Per Serving

Calories 480

Total Fat 8g

Sat Fat 2 g Mono Fat 2 g Poly Fat 1 g

Protein 49 g

Carb 51 g

Fiber 10 g

Cholesterol 80 mg

Sodium 990 mg

Excellent Source of Calcium, Fiber, Folate, Iodine, Iron, Manganese, Protein, Riboflavin, Vitamin A, Vitamin C, Vitamin K.

Good Source of Copper, Niacin, Pantothenic Acid, Phosphorus, Potassium, Selenium, Thiamin, Vitamin B6, Vitamin D.

RATATOUILLE WITH FRESH RED SNAPPER AND HERBED GOAT CHEESE CROSTINI

This dish is inspired by a dinner I had at a lovely little restaurant in Paris, where the food was just the opposite of what you might expect from French cuisine. It was uncomplicated, with clean, clear flavors and a modern lightness. In this take on the classic eggplant, zucchini, and tomato stew, each vegetable is finely diced and cooked just enough to be tender while retaining its fresh individuality. It makes a scrumptious, luxurious bed for the red snapper fillet.

- 3 tablespoons olive oil
- 1 large eggplant (about 1 pound), trimmed and cut into small dice
- 1 medium onion, cut into small dice
- 2 medium zucchini (1 pound total), trimmed and cut into small dice
- 2 cloves garlic, minced
- 1 (14.5-ounce) can no-salt-added diced tomatoes
- teaspoon herbes de Provence, or ½ teaspoon dried thyme and ¼ teaspoon each of dried rosemary and dried marjoram
- ¾ teaspoon salt, plus more to taste
- ½ teaspoon freshly ground black pepper
- ¼ cup chopped fresh basil, plus more for garnish
- 4 (5-ounce) red snapper fillets, skin-on
- 2 teaspoons fresh lemon juice

In a large nonstick skillet, heat 1 tablespoon of olive oil over medium-high heat. Add the eggplant and cook, stirring, until softened, about 5 minutes. Remove the eggplant from the skillet. Heat another tablespoon of oil in the same skillet over medium-high heat. Add the onion and cook, stirring, until softened, about 5 minutes. Add the zucchini and garlic to the pan and cook, stirring occasionally, until the zucchini is softened, 6 minutes. Return the eggplant to the pan and add the tomatoes, herbes de Provence, ½ teaspoon of the salt, and ¼ teaspoon of the pepper. Simmer for 10 minutes. Season with more salt to taste. Stir in ¼ cup of the basil and remove from the heat.

Preheat the broiler. Sprinkle the fillets with the remaining ¼ teaspoon each of salt and pepper. Combine the remaining 1 tablespoon of olive oil with the lemon juice and brush on the fillets. Broil until the fish is cooked and firm, about 7 minutes.

Mound 1 cup of the ratatouille onto 4 plates and top each with 1 fish fillet. Garnish with basil. Serve with the crostini.

Makes 4 servings

Serving Size

1 cup ratatouille, 1 fish fillet, and 2 pieces crostini

Per Serving

Calories 420

Total Fat 17 g

Sat Fat 4.5 g Mono Fat 9 g Poly Fat 2.5 g

Protein 40 g

Carb 30 g

Fiber 9 g

Cholesterol 60 mg

Sodium 770 mg

Excellent Source of Copper, Fiber, Folate, Magnesium, Manganese, Phosphorus, Potassium, Protein, Selenium, Vitamin A, Vitamin B6, Vitamin B12, Vitamin C, Vitamin K.

Good Source of Calcium, Iron, Niacin, Pantothenic Acid, Riboflavin, Thiamin, Zinc.

HERBED GOAT CHEESE CROSTINI

Just about any toasted cheese and bread combination is a winner to me. But this one is a standout, with the aroma of herbs and garlic and warm creamy cheese atop the crunch of baguette. It is easy enough to make just for you but has an elegant flair that makes it worthy of company.

- 8 ½-inch-thick slices whole-wheat baguette

- 1 large clove garlic
- 2 ounces herbed goat cheese (chevre)
- Preheat the broiler.

Place the bread slices on a baking tray. Cut the garlic clove in half and rub the top of each slice of bread well with the cut side of the garlic clove. Spread ¼ ounce of the goat cheese on each slice of bread. Broil until the bread is toasted and the cheese is warmed and lightly browned.

Makes 4 servings

Serving Size

2 pieces

SALMON MARIANTED IN TOMATO SAUCE WITH SWISS CHARD

What do you get when you top a pile of tender greens with ajuicy fillet of fish, smother them with the most wonderfully fragrant and flavorful sauce, and let them simmer, soften, and meld together in the oven? A meal that lights up your taste buds and warms your belly, heart, and soul.

- tablespoon olive oil
- 4 cloves garlic, minced
- (14.5-ounce) can no-salt-added diced tomatoes
- 1 (12-ounce) can no-salt-added tomato sauce
- 1 (7-ounce) jar roasted red peppers, drained, rinsed, and thinly sliced
- dried whole red chile peppers
- 1 teaspoon ground cumin
- ½ teaspoon ground coriander
- ½ teaspoon salt
- ½ teaspoon freshly ground black pepper
- 1 large bunch Swiss chard, washed well and dried, tough center stems removed, coarsely chopped (about 8 cups)
- (6-ounce) skinless salmon fillets
- ¼ cup chopped cilantro
- cups cooked whole-grain couscous

Preheat the oven to 350°F. Heat the oil in a large skillet over medium- low heat. Add the garlic and cook, stirring, until softened and golden, about 1 minute. Add the diced tomatoes withjuice, tomato sauce, red peppers, chili peppers, cumin, coriander, and V! teaspoon each of salt and pepper. Bring to a boil, then reduce the heat to medium-low and simmer until the sauce thickens slightly, about 10 minutes. Remove from the heat and remove and discard the chile peppers.

Place the Swiss chard on the bottom of a 9x 13-inch glass baking dish. Season the fish fillets with the remaining ¼ teaspoon each of salt and pepper and place on top of the chard. Top with the sauce and bake, covered, until the fish is just cooked and the chard is wilted, about 15 minutes. Remove the cover and bake for an additional 5 minutes.

Sprinkle with cilantro and serve over couscous.

Makes 4 servings

Serving Size

1 salmon fillet, ¾ cup chard and sauce, and ¾ cup couscous

Per Serving

Calories 520

Total Fat 16 g

Sat Fat 2.5 g Mono Fat 6 g Poly Fat 5.5 g

Protein 43 g

Carb 48 g

Fiber 7 g

Cholesterol 95 mg

Sodium 700 mg

Excellent Source of Copper, Fiber, Folate, Iron, Magnesium, Manganese, Niacin, Pantothenic Acid, Phosphorus, Potassium, Protein, Riboflavin, Selenium, Thiamin, Vitamin A, Vitamin B6, Vitamin B12, Vitamin C, Vitamin 0, Vitamin K .

Good Source of Calcium, Zinc.

SALMON MILANESE WITH QUINOA PILAF

This dish is as impressive looking as it is delicious and nutrient packed. It is a two-tiered wonder with a buttery salmon base and flavorful spinach topping. It is a special preparation that takes no special skill or effort to make.

- 2 (10-ounce) packages frozen spinach, thawed
- 1 tablespoon olive oil
- ¼ cup minced shallots
- 2 teaspoons minced garlic
- 5 sun-dried tomatoes, chopped
- ¼ teaspoon crushed red pepper flakes
- ½ teaspoon salt, plus more to taste
- ¼ teaspoon freshly ground black pepper, plus more to taste
- ½ cup part-skim ricotta cheese
- 4 (6-ounce) skinless salmon fillets, rinsed and patted dry

Preheat the oven to 350°F. Using your hands, squeeze all excess liquid from the spinach.

Heat the olive oil in a large skillet over medium heat. Add the shallots and cook, stirring, until they begin to soften, about 3 minutes. Add the garlic and cook for 1 minute more. Add the spinach, sun-dried tomatoes, red pepper flakes, salt, and pepper and cook, stirring, for an additional 2 minutes. Remove from the heat and let cool for approximately 15 minutes. Add the ricotta and stir to combine. Season with additional salt and pepper to taste.

Using your hands, pack approximately ½ cup of the spinach mixture on top of each salmon fillet, forming the mixture to the shape of the fillet. Place the fillets on a rimmed baking sheet or in a glass baking dish and bake for 15 minutes, until the salmon is cooked through.

Serve alongside the pilaf.

Makes 4 servings

Serving Size

1 piece salmon and 1 cup pilaf

Per Serving

Calories 610

Total Fat 25 g

Sat Fat 4.5 g Mono Fat 10 g Poly Fat 8 g

Protein 54 g

Carb 43 g

Fiber 8 g

Cholesterol 100 mg

Sodium 640 mg

Excellent Source of Calcium, Copper, FIBER, Folate, iron, Magnesium, Manganese, Niacin, Phosphorus, Potassium, Protein, Riboflavin, Selenium, Thiamin, Vitamin A, Vitamin B6, Vitamin C, Vitamin D, Vitamin K, Zinc.

Good Source of Pantothenic Acid.

DESSERTS-IN A FLASH

These desserts are so fabulous, yet so quick and simple, making them is like making magic. They are sweet treats you can whip up fast but you'll want to eat nice and slow, savoring every bite.

SWEET COMBO CLUSTER

The combination of crunchy toasted almonds and chewy sweet-tart cherries covered in rich dark chocolate is about as close to the definition of "pure pleasure" as you can possibly get. Close your eyes as you eat one for the maximum effect.

- 1 cup whole roasted almonds, coarsely chopped
- ½ cup dried cherries, coarsely chopped
- 6 ounces dark or bittersweet chocolate (60% to 70% cocoa solids), finely chopped

In a medium bowl, toss together the almonds and cherries. Line a baking sheet with wax paper.

Melt half of the chocolate in the top of a double boiler over slightly simmering water, over the lowest possible heat, stirring frequently; make sure the water is not touching the top pan. Remove the double boiler from the heat, and stir in the rest of the chocolate until melted. Remove the top pan with the chocolate in it, gently wipe the bottom of it, and set it aside for a moment. Replace the simmering water in the bottom pan with warm tap water. Put the pan of melted chocolate on top of the warm water. This will keep the chocolate at the right temperature while you make the clusters.

Stir the fruit/nut mixture into the chocolate. Spoon out heaping tablespoon-size clusters of the chocolate mixture onto the baking sheet about 1 inch apart. Put them in the refrigerator to cool and set for about 20 minutes. Store and serve at room temperature.

Makes 12 servings

Serving Size

1 cluster

Per Serving

Calories 150

Total Fat 10 g

Sat Fat 3 g Mono Fat 4 g

Poly Fat 1.5 g Protein 4 g

Carb 15 g

Fiber 2 g

Cholesterol 0 mg

Sodium 5 mg

Good Source of Manganese.

DRIED FRUIT WITH CHOCOLATE TOPPING

Something magical happens when dried fruit meets dark chocolate. Each has its own concentrated and complex flavors that, taken together, amplify and balance one another-a real marriage made in heaven.

- 2 ½ ounces dark or bittersweet chocolate (60% to 70% cocoa solids), chopped
- 8 ounces mixed dried fruit (such as pears, apricots, mango, and crystallized ginger)

Line a baking sheet with wax paper.

Place the chocolate in the top of a double boiler set over barely simmering water. Make sure the bottom of the pan does not touch the water. Melt the chocolate, stirring frequently, for about 1 minute.

Remove the pan from the heat.

Dip each piece of fruit into the chocolate so that half of the piece is coated with chocolate. Place on the wax paper and place in the refrigerator to cool and set, about 20 minutes. Store and serve at room temperature.

Makes 6 servings

Serving Size

3 pieces

Per Serving

Calories 160

Total Fat 4 g

Sat Fat 2.5 g Mono Fat 0 g Poly Fat 0 g

Protein 1 g

Carb 31 g

Fiber 2 g

Cholesterol 0 mg

Sodium 15 mg

Good Source of Vitamin A.

POWDERED COCONUT-SUGAR CRISPS

If you are craving something crunchy and sweet, these treats are the perfect solution. They are fun to experiment with too. Try a sprinkle of cinnamon or cocoa or cut them into different shapes with a cookie cutter, an especially fun project with kids.

- 2 teaspoons canola oil
- cooking spary
- 1 teaspoon of coconut-sugar
- 10 wonton wrappers

Makes 4 servings

Serving Size

5 crisps

Per Serving

Calories 80

Total Fat 2.5 g Sat Fat 0 g Mono Fat 1.5 g

Poly Fat 0 g

Protein 3 g

Carb 14 g

Fiber 0 g

Cholesterol 0 mg

Sodium 115 mg

Preheat the oven to 375°F. Spray a baking sheet with the cooking spray.

Cut the wonton wrappers in half on the diagonal so you wind up with 20 triangles. In a medium-size bowl, toss the triangles gently with the canola oil, separating the pieces gently so each piece is coated with oil.

Place the triangles on the baking sheet in a single layer. Bake for about 10 minutes, until they are golden brown and crisped.

Dust with confectioners' sugar and serve. Crisps will keep up to 4 days in an airtight container.

CHOCOLATE-COVERED CHEESE PANINI BITES

Chocolate, cream cheese, and raspberry jam melted together on crusty bread-yum ! It's not exactly health food but it's testament to my philosophy that no food is offlimits. Sometimes a little of what you crave is exactly what you need to hit the spot and move on. These are mini bites of maximum satisfaction.

- Cooking spray
- ½ loaf ciabatta or other Italian bread (about 6 ounces, 8x4 inches)

- ¼ cup (2 ounces) Neufchatel cheese (reduced-fat cream cheese), softened
- 2 ounces dark or bittersweet chocolate (60% to 70% cocoa solids), coarsely chopped
- 2 tablespoons raspberry jam

Slice the bread open and spread one side evenly with cream cheese. Distribute the chocolate evenly on top of the cream cheese. Spread the other side of the bread with jam and close the bread to make a sandwich.

Spray a large cast-iron or nonstick skillet with cooking spray and heat over medium-high heat. Place the bread in the pan. Cover it with another smaller, heavy skillet and weigh it down with a heavy can.

Cook until the underside of the bread is well toasted, 3 to 4 minutes. Flip and cook until the chocolate is melted and the other side of the bread is browned, about 3 more minutes. Remove from the heat and slice into 8 equal-size pieces.

Makes 4 servings

Serving Size

2 pieces

Per Serving

Calories 250

Total Fat 11 g

Sat Fat 5 g Mono Fat 1 g

Poly Fat 0.5 g

Protein 6 g

Carb 35 g

Fiber 2 g

Cholesterol 10 mg

Sodium 300 mg

Excellent Source of Folate.

Good Source of Protein, Selenium, Thiamin .

HONEYDEW SOUP WITH LEMON-RASPBERRY SORBET

Fresh, cool, and colorful, this elegant dessert is special enough for company but quick and simple enough for every day.

- 5 cups tightly packed honeydew chunks (from half of a 6 ½ -pound honeydew, peeled and seeded)
- 1 tablespoon honey
- 2 tablespoons fresh lime juice
- ½ cup unsweetened light coconut milk
- 1 cup raspberry sorbet
- 2 teaspoons finely chopped fresh mint

In a food processor, puree the honeydew, honey, and lime juice. Pour into a bowl and stir in the coconut milk. The soup will keep in the refrigerator in an airtight container for up to 4 days.

To serve, ladle the soup into 4 shallow soup plates. Place a scoop of raspberry sorbet in the center of each serving and top with the chopped mint.

Makes 4 servings

Serving Size

1 cup of soup and ¼ cup scoop of sorbet

Per Serving

Calories 170

Total Fat 2 g

Sat Fat 1.5 g Mono Fat 0 g Poly Fat 0 g

Protein 2 g

Carb 40 g

Fiber 3 g

Cholesterol 0 mg

Sodium 45 mg

Excellent Source of Vitamin C.

Good Source of Fiber, Folate, Potassium.

ORANGES DIPPED IN HONEY WITH TOASTED HAZELNUTS

Gorgeous, juicy orange slices are given the royal treatment here, dressed in a golden, rosemary-infused, honey-lemon syrup and crowned with a sprinkle of rich hazelnuts. It is a perfect finish for a hearty autumn or winter dinner.

- 3 tablespoons hazelnuts
- ¼ cup honey
- 4 teaspoons fresh lemon juice
- 1 sprig fresh rosemary, plus more sprigs for garnish
- 4 navel oranges

Place the hazelnuts in a dry skillet and toast over medium-high heat, stirring frequently, until fragrant and light brown, about 3 minutes. Allow to cool, then roughly chop.

Place the honey, lemon juice, and 1 rosemary sprig in a small saucepan and bring to a boil. Remove from the heat and let the rosemary steep for 10 minutes, or up to 1 hour, then remove the rosemary sprig.

Slice off the tops and bottoms of the oranges, then slice down the sides of the oranges, removing the skin and the white pith. Slice each orange into 4 or 5 rings and place in a bowl or on a serving plate. Stir the juice that accumulated from cutting the oranges into the honey-lemon mixture.

To serve, drizzle the orange slices with the honey-lemon mixture. Top with the hazelnuts and garnish with additional rosemary sprigs.

Makes 4 servings

Serving Size

orange slices, 1 ½ tablespoons honey mixture, 2 teaspoons hazelnuts

Per Serving

Calories 180

Total Fat 4 g

Sat Fat 0 g Mono Fat 3 g Poly Fat 0.5 g

Protein 3 g

Carb 37 g

Fiber 4 g

Cholesterol 0 mg

Sodium 0 mg

Excellent Source of Manganese, Vitamin C

Good Source of Fiber, Folate

SPICY PINEAPPLE

This fun-to-eat sugar dip brings out the best in the sweet, tangy pineapple and leaves you with an exciting, warm tingle on your tongue.

- 1/3 cup sugar
- 1 ½ teaspoons chili powder
- 1 teaspoon salt
- 1 pineapple, peeled, cored, and cut into 1 ½ -inch chunks (about 3 cups)
- 6 (6-inch) wooden skewers

Combine the sugar, chili powder, and salt in a dry, small bowl and stir to incorporate. Place in a shallow serving dish. Thread 3 pineapple chunks onto each skewer. Arrange the skewers on a serving dish and serve with the sugar dip.

Makes 6 servings

Serving Size

3 pineapple chunks and 1 tablespoon sugar dip

Per Serving

Calories 70

Total Fat 0 g

Sat Fat 0 g Mono Fat 0 g Poly Fat 0 g

Protein 0 g

Carb 19 g

Fiber 1 g

Cholesterol 0 mg

Sodium 390 mg

Excellent Source of Manganese, Vitamin C.

PEARS DIPPED IN ALMOND CREAM

This rich, subtly tangy cream spiked with almond essence gives ripe, sliced pearsjust the embellishment they need to go from fruit to fabulous.

- ¼ cup sliced almonds
- ½ up heavy whipping cream
- 2 tablespoons confectioners' sugar
- ½ cup plain Greek-style nonfat yogurt
- ¾ teaspoon almond extract
- 4 firm ripe pears

Toast the almonds in a dry skillet over medium-high heat, stirring frequently, until golden brown and fragrant, about 2 minutes.

Whip the cream with an electric beater until it is thickened. Add the sugar and continue beating until soft peaks are formed. Gently fold in the yogurt and almond extract. The cream will keep in the refrigerator, covered, for 2 days.

Core and slice the pears and arrange slices of half a pear on each serving plate. Top each with 3 tablespoons of the cream and sprinkle with almonds.

Makes 8 servings

Serving Size

½ pear, 3 tablespoons cream, and ½ tablespoon almonds

Per Serving

Calories 140

Total Fat 7 g

Sat Fat 3.5 g Mono Fat 2.5 g Poly Fat 0.5 g

Protein 3 g

Carb 17 g

Fiber 3 g

Cholesterol 20 mg

Sodium 10 mg

Good Source of Fiber.

FRUIT SALAD WITH MINT AND HONEY-LIME DRESSING

Honey, mint, and a hit of lime give this multicolored fruit salad a bold flavor punch.

- 1/3 cantaloupe, peeled, seeded, and cut into ¾ -inch chunks (about 2 cups)
- 1 (1 6-ounce) container fresh strawberries, quartered (about 3 cups)
- 4 medium kiwifruit, peeled and cut into ¾ -inch chunks (about 2 ½ cups)
- 3 tablespoons fresh lime juice
- 3 tablespoons fresh mint leaves, finely chopped
- 3 tablespoons honey
- 1 teaspoon freshly grated lime zest

Place all of the fruit in a large bowl. In a small bowl, whisk together the lime juice, mint, honey, and zest. Right before serving, pour the dressing over the fruit and toss gently to combine.

Makes 6 servings

Serving Size

1 cup

Per Serving

Calories 110

Total Fat 0.5 g

Sat Fat 0 g Mono Fat 0 g Poly Fat 0 g

Protein 4 g

Carb 27 g

Fiber 4 g

Sodium 10 mg

Cholesterol 0 mg

Excellent Source of Vitamin A, Vitamin C, Vitamin K.

Good Source of Fiber, Folate, Manganese, Potassium.

Did You Know?

This fruit salad could help your skin look younger! That's because it is an excellent source of both vitamin C and beta carotene (a form of vitamin A) , which can help shield skin from the aging effects of the sun and pollution.

BBQ PEACHES WITH ICE CREAM

Grilling fruit makes it more decadent by intensifying its flavor, warming and plumping it. A little ice cream and a sprig of mint where the pit once was make these peaches a lovely finish to a summer meal.

- 4 ripe but firm peaches
- 2 teaspoons canola oil
- ½ cup light vanilla ice cream or frozen yogurt
- 8 small sprigs fresh mint

Preheat a grill or nonstick grill pan over medium heat.

Cut each peach in half and remove the pits. Brush the cut side of each peach half with oil. Place the peaches cut side down on the grill or grill pan and cook until the peaches soften slightly and grill marks are formed, 2 to 3 minutes.

Place a tablespoon-size scoop of ice cream in the center of each peach half. Garnish with mint and serve.

Makes 4 servings

Serving Size

peach halves

Per Serving

Calories 91

Total Fat 3.5 g

Sat Fat 0.5 g Mono Fat 1.75 g Poly Fat 0.75 g

Protein 3 g

Carb 13 g

Fiber 1 g

Cholesterol 5 mg

Sodium 10 mg

Good Source of Vitamin C.

FAST CAKE WITH MANGO SAUCE

This vibrant yellow mango sauce is the perfect balance of sweet and tangy. Here it turns ordinary store-bought cake into a magnificent dessert, but it also happens to be delicious over ice cream. All it takes is a quick whir of the blender.

- 2 medium ripe mangoes, peeled, pitted, and cut into chunks, or one (10 ounce) bag frozen mango, thawed
- 2 tablespoons fresh lime juice 1 tablespoon sugar
- 2 teaspoons Cointreau or other orange liqueur, optional 1 store-bought angel food cake (about 13 ounces)
- ¼ cup fresh mint leaves

In a blender or food processor, process half the mangoes with the lime juice, sugar, and Cointreau until smooth. Dice the rest of the mangoes.

Slice the cake, pour 1 tablespoon of the mango sauce over each slice, and toss some diced mango on top. Garnish with the mint leaves and serve.

Makes 12 servings

Serving Size

1 slice cake, 1 tablespoon sauce, and 1 tablespoon mango chunks

Per Serving

Calories 11

Total Fat 0 g

Sat Fat 0 g Mono Fat 0 g Poly Fat 0 g

Protein 2 g

Carb 25 g

Fiber 1 g

Cholesterol 0 mg

Sodium 230 mg

Good Source of Riboflavin, Vitamin C.

DESSERTS-EXTRA SPECIAL

There is something to be said for anticipation-waiting for a cobbler to come out of the oven as the aroma teases you, looking forward to the glorious moment when a silky pudding is set or decadent chocolate pops are frozen. Something about the waiting makes the digging in even more satisfying. These scrumptious desserts may ask you to wait a bit, but they won't ask you to do much more than that, except enjoy.

CRISPY RICE TREATS WITH DRIED FRUITS

Sticky sweet squares of crispy rice make you feel like a kid again- when you are making them and when you are eating them. Here the family favorite is updated, with whole-grain cereal and peanut butter and honey instead of marshmallow. I added chewy, tangy dried cherries to the mix here, but it works with any dried fruit-or even chocolate chips.

- ¾ cup chunky natural-style peanut butter
- ¾ cup honey
- 6 cups crispy brown rice cereal
- 2/3 cup (3 ounces) dried cherries, chopped Cooking spray

Combine the peanut butter and honey in a large pot and heat over medium-low heat until melted, 2 to 3 minutes. Add the brown rice cereal and cherries and stir to combine until the mixture is sticky. Press into a 9x 1 3-inch pan sprayed with cooking spray. Chill in the refrigerator for 40 minutes. Cut into fifteen 2 V2x3-inch squares.

Makes 15 servings

Serving Size

1 square

Per Serving

Calories 210

Total Fat 7 g

Sat Fat 1.5 g Mono Fat 3 g Poly Fat 1. 5 g

Protein 5 g

Carb 32 g

Fiber 2 g

Cholesterol 0 mg

Sodium 65 mg

AROMATIC TRUFFLES WITH FIGS

Fig and ginger are a fabulous duo, with ginger adding just the right zing to the earthy sweet fruit. But when you envelop those flavors in rich dark chocolate-look out! Because then you have "fabulous" plus chocolate. Need I say more?

- 2 cups dried black Mission figs or other dried figs (about 8 ounces)
- ½ cup crystallized ginger (about 2 ounces)
- 1 tablespoon honey
- ½ teaspoon ground cinnamon
- 2 ½ ounces dark chocolate (60% to 70% cocoa solids) , chopped

Remove the stems from the figs and discard. Put the figs, ginger, honey, and cinnamon in a food processor and process for about 45 seconds, until the ingredients are finely chopped and begin to stick together. Roll the fig mixture with your hands into heaping teaspoon- size balls and set them on a baking sheet or plate lined with wax paper.

Place a small bowl over a saucepan containing barely simmering water over low heat. Make sure the water is at least 2 inches from the bottom of the bowl. Place half the chocolate in the bowl and stir until it is melted. Remove the saucepan from the heat and add the remaining chocolate. Stir until all the chocolate is melted. Remove the bowl containing the chocolate from the pan.

Roll the fig balls in the melted chocolate, one or two at a time, until they are all covered. Place them back on the wax paper and then chill in the refrigerator until set, about 15 minutes. Serve at room temperature.

Makes 8 servings

Serving Size

2 truffles

Per Serving

Calories 190

Total Fat 3.5 g Sat Fat 2 g Mono Fat 0 g Poly Fat 0 g

Protein 3 g

Carb 47 g

Fiber 8 g

Cholesterol 0 mg

Sodium 5 mg

Excellent Source of Fiber.

Good Source of Manganese.

SIMPLE LEMON BARS

If you love cheesecake and you love lemon, you will double-love these delicious bars. They have a velvety, cream cheese filling with just the right citrus kick and that crave-able, classic graham cracker crust. All that and you don't even need an oven to make them .

- Crust
- 14 whole-grain graham cracker squares (7 full sheets)
- 2 tablespoons melted unsalted butter
- 1 tablespoon dark brown sugar
- ¼ teaspoon salt
- Cooking spray Filling
- 1 (8-ounce) package Neufchatel cheese (reduced-fat cream cheese), softened at room temperature
- 1 (14-ounce) can fat-free sweetened condensed milk
- ¼ cup pasteurized egg product (such as Egg Beaters)
- ½ cup fresh lemon juice
- 1 teaspoon finely grated lemon zest 2 teaspoons powdered gelatin
- 3 tablespoons boiling water

Place the graham crackers in a food processor and pulse until crumbs are formed. Add the butter, brown sugar, and salt and pulse until crumbs resemble wet sand. Coat an 8-inch-square pan with cooking spray and pack the crumbs firmly into the bottom of it. Refrigerate while you prepare the filling.

In a large bowl, combine the cream cheese, condensed milk, and pasteurized egg product and beat on high with an electric mixer until smooth and creamy, about 2 minutes. Add the lemon juice and zest and beat until fully incorporated, another 30 seconds. In a small bowl, combine the gelatin and boiling water and whisk until the gelatin is entirely dissolved; let cool for 2 to 3 minutes. Using a spoon, stir the gelatin into the cream cheese mixture until incorporated. Pour the filling over the crust. Refrigerate for at least 8 hours. Slice into 2-inch squares using a chilled knife coated with cooking spray.

Makes 16 servings

Serving Size

1 square

Per Serving

Calories 160

Total Fat 5 g

Sat Fat 3 g Mono Fat 1.5 g Poly Fat 0.5 g

Protein 3 g

Carb 23 g

Fiber 0 g

Cholesterol 20 mg

Sodium 160 mg

COBBLER WITH LIME-BERRIES

When this down-home dessert comes out of the oven just watch the faces of those around you light up. They'll see flakey golden biscuits sitting proudly atop a bubbling mix of sweetened berries, bursting with juice that has thickened just enough to form a luscious fruit sauce. Eating it will satisfy body and soul. You gotta love a recipe that gives so much for so little effort.

- Cooking spray
- 2 (12-ounce) bags frozen mixed berries, thawed (about 6 cups)
- 4 teaspoons lime juice
- ¼ cup whole-wheat flour
- ¼ cup sugar
- Finely grated zest of 1 orange (about 2 teaspoons)
- Topping
- ¼ cup whole-wheat flour
- ¼ cup all-purpose flour
- 2 tablespoons plus
- 1 teaspoon sugar
- ½ teaspoon baking powder
- ¼ teaspoon baking soda
- ¼ teaspoon salt
- 2 tablespoons chilled unsalted butter, cut into small pieces
- 1/3 cup low-fat buttermilk
- 2 tablespoons canola oil

Preheat the oven to 400°F. Coat an 8x8-inch baking dish with cooking spray.

In a large bowl, toss the berries with the whole-wheat flour, sugar, and zest. Transfer the berry mixture to the baking dish and set aside.

In a medium bowl, whisk together the flours, 2 tablespoons of the sugar, baking powder, baking soda, and salt. Cut in the butter using 2 knives or a pastry cutter until many small pebble-size pieces are formed.

In a small bowl or pitcher, whisk together the buttermilk and oil. Add the mixture to the dry ingredients and mix until just moistened. Do not over mix. Drop the batter onto the fruit, forming 6 mounds. Sprinkle with the remaining teaspoon of sugar. Bake for 30 minutes, until the fruit is bubbly and the top is golden. Let stand for at least 10 minutes before serving.

Makes 6 servings

Serving Size

¾ cup

Per Serving

Calories 230

Total Fat 10g

Sat Fat 3 g Mono Fat 4 g Poly Fat 1.5 g

Protein 4 g

Carb 36 g

Fiber 5 g

Cholesterol 10 mg

Sodium 210 mg

Excellent Source of Vitamin C.

Good Source of Fiber, Manganese, Selenium.

BIG APPLE

With a sweet, tender apple "filling" and a golden buttery crust made from fresh bread crumbs, this dish gives you all the homey flavors and aromas of an apple pie, but without the fuss.

- 5 large Golden Delicious apples (about 2 pounds) , peeled and thinly sliced
- 1 cup apple cider
- 3 tablespoons brown sugar
- 1 teaspoon vanilla extract
- 1 teaspoon ground cinnamon
- 2 tablespoons unsalted butter
- 3 slices whole-wheat bread (1 ounce each; crusts included) , or enough to make about 2 ¼ cups crumbs
- 3 tablespoons chopped walnuts Preheat the oven to 350°F.

Combine the apples, apple cider, 1 tablespoon of the brown sugar, the vanilla, and ½ teaspoon of the cinnamon in a large saucepan over medium-high heat. Cook, stirring occasionally, until the apples are tender but still retain their shape, about 10 minutes. Stir in 1 tablespoon of the butter until melted, remove from the heat, and transfer the apple mixture to a 9-inch pie plate or a ceramic dish.

Place the bread in the food processor and process until crumbs are formed, about 15 seconds. Melt the remaining 1 tablespoon butter in the microwave for 20 seconds. Toss the crumbs with the melted butter, walnuts, remaining 2 tablespoons of brown sugar, and remaining ½ teaspoon of cinnamon. Scatter the crumb mixture on top of the apples and bake for 30 minutes, until the topping is crisped and lightly browned.

Makes 6 servings

Serving Size

1 cup

Per Serving

Calories 240

Total Fat 7 g

Sat Fat 3 g Mono Fat 1.5 g Poly Fat 2 g

Protein 4 g

Carb 42 g

Fiber 6 g

Cholesterol 10 mg

Sodium 75 mg

Excellent Source of Fiber, Manganese.

Good Source of Vitamin C.

RASPBERRY TART

Tart (or clafoutis)is a thick dessert pancake that is chock-full of fruit. It looks so special in its golden brown splendor, studded with plump raspberries and dusted with sugar, your guests will never guess how easy it is to whip up.

- Cooking spray
- 1 tablespoon plus 1/3 cup whole-wheat pastry flour
- 1 ½ cups fresh or frozen (unthawed) raspberries (6 ounces)
- 1 large egg and 2 large egg whites, lightly beaten
- 1 cup low-fat (1 ¾) milk
- ¼ cup granulated sugar
- 1 tablespoon melted butter, cooled
- 1 teaspoon vanilla extract or raspberry liqueur
- ¼ teaspoon salt
- 1 tablespoon turbinado sugar (such as Sugar in the Raw) Preheat the oven to 350°F.

Spray a 9-inch pie plate or ceramic dish with cooking spray and coat with 1 tablespoon of the flour, shaking off the excess. Scatter the raspberries on the surface of the dish and reserve.

In a medium-size bowl, combine the egg and egg whites, milk, granulated sugar, butter, vanilla or liqueur, and salt and whisk to blend. Add the remaining 1/3 cup of flour and stir to incorporate, making sure not to overwork the batter. Pour the batter over the raspberries. Bake until the clafoutis is golden brown and the center is set, 45 to 50 minutes. Sprinkle with the turbinado sugar and serve immediately.

Makes 6 servings

Serving Size

1 wedge

Per Serving

Calories 130

Total Fat 3.5 g

Sat Fat 1.5 g Mono Fat 0.5 g Poly Fat 0 g Protein 5 g

Carb 19 g

Fiber 2 g

Cholesterol 45 mg

Sodium 140 mg

Good Source of Iodine, Thiamin, Vitamin C.

HALLOWEEN PUDDING

This dessert is the magic that happens when creamy rice pudding meets aromatic, deeply flavorful pumpkin pie. It is the best of both familiar favorites, and it practically makes itself in the oven.

- 2 cups water
- 1 cup arborio rice

- 3 cups reduced-fat (2%) milk
- 1 cup solid-pack pure pumpkin (not pumpkin pie filling)
- ¾ cup honey
- teaspoon vanilla extract
- ¾ teaspoon ground cinnamon plus more for garnish
- ¼ teaspoon ground ginger
- ¼ teaspoon ground nutmeg
- ¼ teaspoon salt
- 1/3 cup heavy whipping cream, whipped Preheat the oven to 375°F.

Bring the water to a boil in an ovenproof 4-quart saucepan. Stir in the rice and cover. Reduce the heat to low and simmer until the rice is nearly cooked, about 20 minutes.

In a large bowl, whisk together the milk, pumpkin, honey, vanilla, cinnamon, ginger, nutmeg, and salt. While the rice is still hot, add the pumpkin mixture to the saucepan and stir well to combine. Cover and transfer to the oven. Bake until the liquid has reduced by about a third and the mixture is foamy and bubbling, 45 to 50 minutes. Remove from the oven and stir well to combine all the ingredients. Transfer to a large bowl, then cover and chill in the refrigerator for at least 8 hours or overnight. The pudding will keep for up to 4 days in an airtight container in the refrigerator. Serve with a dollop of whipped cream and a sprinkling of cinnamon.

Makes 8 servings

Serving Size

½ cup rice pudding and 1 ½ tablespoons whipped cream

Per Serving

Calories 250

Total Fat 6 g

Sat Fat 3.5 g Mono Fat 1.5 g Poly Fat 0 g

Protein 5 g

Carb 43 g

Fiber 1 g

Cholesterol 20 mg

Sodium 120 mg

Excellent Source of Vitamin A.

Good Source of Calcium, Iodine, Phosphorus, Riboflavin, Vitamin D.

RICOTTA CREAM WITH STRAWBERRIES SYRUP

Ricotta cheese fitsjust as well in the world of sweet as it does in savory. Whip it up with a little honey and you get the most magnificent, rich cream, which is fantastic topped with juicy strawberries in a sweet balsamic syrup. Ribbons of basil add a fresh perfume, proving it too is delightful in dessert.

- 1 cup part-skim ricotta cheese
- 2 tablespoons honey
- ½ teaspoon vanilla extract
- 3 tablespoons balsamic vinegar
- 2 tablespoons sugar
- (1 6-ounce) container fresh strawberries, stems removed and quartered
- 2 tablespoons fresh basil leaves, cut into ribbons

Put the ricotta cheese, honey, and vanilla extract into the small bowl of a food processor and process until smooth, about 1 minute. Transfer to a small bowl and refrigerate for at least 2 hours.

In a small saucepan, combine the vinegar and sugar and bring to a boil. Simmer over medium heat for 2 minutes, stirring occasionally. Allow to cool completely. In a medium-size bowl, toss the berries with the basil and the balsamic syrup.

Divide the ricotta mixture among 4 cocktail glasses or dessert bowls, top with the berry mixture, and serve.

Makes 4 servings

Serving Size

1/3 cup cream and ½ cup berries

Per Serving

Calories 180

Total Fat 5 g

Sat Fat 3 g

Mono Fat 1.5 g Poly Fat 0 g

Protein 8 g

Carb 27 g

Fiber 2 g

Cholesterol 20 mg

Sodium 80 mg

Excellent Source of Manganese, Vitamin C.

Good Source of Calcium, Phosphorus, Protein, Selenium, Vitamin K.

SPARKLING PEACHES COCKTAIL

Maybe it's the bubbly, but this dessert makes me giddy. It's effervescent, exciting, and practically poetic in its elegant simplicity. Just four little ingredients with big power to impress.

- 5 large ripe peaches, or two 10-ounce bags unsweetened frozen sliced peaches
- 1 (750-ml) bottle Prosecco or other sparkling wine (not an extra-dry variety)
- 1/3 cup superfine sugar
- ½ cup packed basil leaves, sliced into ribbons

If using fresh peaches, bring a 4-quart pot of water to a boil and fill a large bowl with ice water. With a paring knife, slice through each peach skin from end to end, but leave the peach intact. Gently place the peaches in the boiling water and boil for 30 seconds. Transfer the peaches into the ice water for 30 seconds, and then remove them using a slotted spoon. Gently remove the skins from the peaches, then split the peaches in half and remove the pits. Cut each peach into 8 slices.

Pour the Prosecco into a large bowl. Add the sugar and stir gently until dissolved. Add the peach slices and basil and stir to combine. Cover and refrigerate for at least 2 hours and up to 8 hours. Serve the peaches in a bowl with some liquid and basil leaves.

Makes 6 servings

Serving Size

2/3 cup peaches and ½ cup liquid

Per Serving

Calories 210

Total Fat 0 g

Sat Fat 0 g Mono Fat 0 g Poly Fat 0 g

Protein 1 g

Carb 31 g

Fiber 2 g

Cholesterol 0 mg

Sodium 0 mg

C"H"OCO-NUT ON STICK

Chocolate and coconut are one of my all-time favorite combinations. Here they meet as an indulgent ice pop, ready to save the day whenever the craving for cool, sweet, and creamy strikes.

- 1 (13.5-ounce) can unsweetened light coconut milk
- 1 cup low-fat (1 %) milk
- 3 ounces dark or bittersweet chocolate (60% to 70% cocoa solids) , chopped
- 2 tablespoons sugar
- 1 teaspoon vanilla extract

Combine all the ingredients in a saucepan and bring to a boil over medium heat. Reduce to a simmer and whisk until the chocolate is melted. Remove from the heat and allow to cool for about 15 minutes. Distribute among six 8-ounce Popsicle molds or paper cups and place in the freezer. If using paper cups, place a Popsicle stick in the center of each cup after a V2 hour in the freezer. Allow to freeze completely, about 4 hours.

Makes 6 servings

Serving Size

1 popsicle

Per Serving

Calories 150 g

Total Fat 8 g

Sat Fat 7 g Mono Fat 1.5 g Poly Fat 0 g

Protein 4 g

Carb 19 g

Fiber 1 g

Cholesterol 0 mg

Sodium 35 mg

SUMMER-VIBES POPS

I came up with this recipe as a kitschy red, white, and blue tribute to Independence Day. They were such a hit with kids and adults alike and so easy to prepare that I wound up making them all summer long. They are the perfect refreshment on a hot day.

- 3 cups cubed seeded watermelon (from about 2 pounds with the rind)
- 2 tablespoons fresh lime juice
- 2 tablespoons confectioner's sugar 1 cup blueberries

Puree the watermelon, lime juice, and sugar in a blender.

Distribute the blueberries among six 8-ounce Popsicle molds or paper cups, then fill each with the watermelon mixture and place in the freezer. If using paper cups, place a Popsicle stick in the center of each cup after a ½ hour in the freezer. Allow to freeze completely, about 4 hours.

Makes 6 servings

Serving Size

1 pop

Per Serving

Calories 45

Total Fat 0 g

Sat Fat 0 g Mono Fat 0 g Poly Fat 0 g

Protein 0 g

Carb 13 g

Fiber 1 g

Cholesterol 0 mg

Sodium 0 mg

Good Source of Vitamin C.

ICE CREAM PACKED

What's more fun than an ice cream sandwich? Mini ice cream sandwiches! They are cold, creamy, crunchy morsels you can eat in two bites. A whimsical treat that is great for a party, or when you just feel like you need one.

- ½ cup light vanilla ice cream or frozen yogurt, softened at room temperature
- 24 vanilla wafer cookies (1 1 inches in diameter)
- 1 ounce dark or bittersweet chocolate (60% to 70% cocoa solids) , finely chopped

Line a shallow storage container with wax paper. Put a small scoop of ice cream (about 2 teaspoons) on a cookie and top with another cookie. Roll the ice cream sandwich in the chopped chocolate so the chocolate adheres to the ice cream. Place in the wax paper-lined container. Repeat with the remaining ingredients until you have 12 ice cream sandwiches.

Cover and place in the freezer to set for at least 30 minutes, or freeze for up to 1 week.

Makes 4 servings

Serving Size

3 ice cream sandwiches

Per Serving

Calories 220

Total Fat 8 g

Sat Fat 3 g Mono Fat 0 g Poly Fat 0 g

Protein 4 g

Carb 35 g

Fiber 1 g

Cholesterol 10 mg

Sodium 170 mg

Printed in Poland
by Amazon Fulfillment
Poland Sp. z o.o., Wrocław